The Arnold and Caroline Rose Monograph Series
of the American Sociological Association

The methodology of Herbert Blumer

See page 107
for other books in the
ASA Rose Monograph Series.

The methodology of Herbert Blumer

Critical interpretation and repair

Kenneth Baugh, Jr

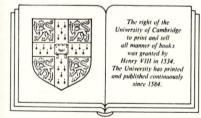

The right of the
University of Cambridge
to print and sell
all manner of books
was granted by
Henry VIII in 1534.
The University has printed
and published continuously
since 1584.

Cambridge University Press

Cambridge
New York   Port Chester   Melbourne   Sydney

Published by the Press Syndicate of the University of Cambridge
The Pitt Building, Trumpington Street, Cambridge CB2 1RP
40 West 20th Street, New York, NY 10011, USA
10 Stamford Road, Oakleigh, Melbourne 3166, Australia

First published 1990

Printed in the United States of America

Library of Congress Cataloging-in-Publication Data
Baugh, Kenneth
The Methodology of Herbert Blumer: critical interpretation and
repair/ Kenneth Baugh, Jr.
p. cm. – (The Arnold and Caroline Rose monograph series of
the American Sociological Association)
Includes bibliographical references.
ISBN 0-521-38246-7
1. Blumer, Herbert, 1900–1987. 2. Sociology – United States.
3. Sociology – Methodology. I. Title. II. Series.
HM22.U68563   1990
301′.072′073 – dc20   89-38447
                                                    CIP

British Library Cataloguing-in-Publication Data
Baugh Kenneth
The methodology of Herbert Blumer: critical interpretation
and repair. – (Arnold and Caroline Rose monograph series
of the American Sociological Association)
1. Sociology. Methodology
I. Title II. Series
301′01′8

ISBN 0-521-38246-7 hard covers

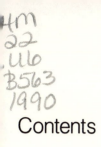

Contents

v

Acknowledgments

Without invoking an entire history, I must mention some specific debts that this work has incurred.

From Florida State University's Department of Philosophy I want to thank Professor David Gruender for his diligence and effectiveness as a critic of an early draft of my argument.

I want also to thank the reviewers of the Rose series for their suggestions and objections. In responding to these, or deciding not to, I have reached the present version of this study.

K. B.

Preface: The standpoint of reading

This study is an interpretation of Herbert Blumer's methodology. As such, it is formed and informed by two distinct sources: a topic, Blumer's methodology, and an approach to that topic, interpretation. Whatever the topic may be in and of itself, here it appears only through interpretation, as interpretation. Any determinations constitutive of interpretation are therefore constitutive of the interpreted topic. More specifically, the assumptions and tendencies which interpretation inevitably *brings* to its topic predelineate the possibilities of construal, fore-favoring some constructions while forestalling others. With that in mind, I want to introduce this study by identifying some interpretive decisions which make my reading of Blumer what it is and not something else.

The first order of interpretive business is simply to locate the topic. Since Blumer's methodology is sited in an indefinite body of discourse, some limits must be set. My choice is to use only Blumer's publicly available texts. The special suitability of this choice lies in the balance it permits between deference and criticism: It at once allows a thinker to present ideas in a considered and deliberate form without thereby collapsing interpretive insight into authorial testimony. As a material witness a text can raise claims of its own over and sometimes against its author, provided, of course, that an interpreter is prepared to hear.

With Blumer's texts in hand, the question arises as to how the task of reading is to be done. Essentially, this task is that of placing texts within a context such that, in a seamless union of the two, a definite meaning is envisaged. The decision here is simply: What context? I will present my answer by critically working through some familiar alternatives.

For the most part, the Blumer secondary literature has approached the question of context from a limited range of choices. In the first case, Blumer's meaning has been determined by reference to his intention, that is, what he had in mind to convey. Interpretation thus directed assumes form as intellectual biography, autobiography, or simply repetitive authorial commentary, all of which accord thematic primacy to the self-understanding of an author.[1] In the second case, Blumer's meaning has been found by reference to his milieu of influences. Here interpretation becomes intellectual history, recovering not merely the author's thought, but such thought in relation to its world, charting the derivations and adaptations which mark all ideas as a child of their time. In the third case, Blumer's meaning has been found within the texts themselves, which in this case become their own context. Focusing immanently upon the textual language, interpretation becomes summary or synopsis, attempting to restate a body of writings in a condensed or miniaturized version.

Despite their differences, all three ways of reading exemplify the same underlying tendency, which is to regard Blumer's meaning as a discrete episode within the history of discourse. So oriented, the job of interpretation consists in recovering the dicourse event, that is, in retrieving and repeating it. This holds equally true whether the event is conceived by reference to an author's intention, a milieu of influences, or textual language alone; in each case the aim is *recovery*.

Such reading stands in marked contrast to the approach to meaning embodied in the working orientation of a methodologist. The methodologist's focus of attention is upon a theme, problem, or issue – in general, upon a subject matter – with which thinking grapples in an effort to reach adequate characterization and resolution. But the subject matter does not give itself easily; thought must wrest it from concealment. In this effort one methodologist may be more successful than another, grasping the latter's work in a critical and corrective way. And as methodology is not a terminal point in itself, but rather exists to guide the conduct of inquiry, methodological principles reach fulfillment in an indefinite horizon of application.

Taken together, these things – the thinking toward a subject matter which exists in concealment and in whose deconcealment and application others may effectively participate – specify the ways in which methodology exists as a contemporaneousness of *renewal*. Such renewal comprises the context of meaning, and some implications of that context, of methodological thought *qua* methodological. By comparison with this context, the reading whose goal is recovery of a discrete historical episode of discourse omits precisely what is most essential. It is not an author's intention, a mileau of influences, or immanent textual language that makes a thought methodological, but simply a certain kind of responsiveness to a certain subject matter.

In this study I want to approach Blumer from a methodological orientation. This means, first and foremost, that the context for placing his texts is their subject matter. Insofar as the subject matter is real and not a figment of Blumer's imagination, it can be identified and dealt with by an indefinite number of persons. Thus, I invoke various thinkers without regard for historical connections to Blumer, requiring only that their ideas help to open up the topic. I also suggest new applications for some of Blumer's ideas. To the extent that the subject matter is in these ways developed independently of Blumer, contextualizing his writings by reference to it produces an interpretation which is *inherently* critical. This becomes particularly patent in those places where the themes I introduce subsume the verbatim of Blumer's texts, but a critical perspective is present throughout.

Most of this study is occupied with textual particulars of Blumer's work as they are taken hold of by my interpretive categories. The outcome of this exercise is to provide the basic gist of Blumer's position. Once that position is in sight, I take issue with it in matters where I believe Blumer is most clearly mistaken. Arguing against him frequently takes the form of further explication of the themes and issues in which Blumer's position has been critically cast; in this way criticism merely continues the work of construal. Finally, moving beyond the mistakes, I make suggestions as to how Blumer's position might be revised and developed to correct some of its errors, though my suggestions in no way constitute a comprehensive treatment of the issues involved. To the extent that correction is the place from which criticism speaks, discussion of the one flows naturally into the other. In every case the specific expository allocation of the moments of my reading is not mechanical but entirely dependent upon the needs of the topic.

Such, then, is what this study is, a "critical interpretation and repair." It is *not* an intellectual biography of Blumer. It is *not* a history of symbolic interactionism. It is *not* an attempt to relate Blumer to pragmatist philosophy (whether conjunctively or disjunctively). It is *not* a sociology of symbolic interactionism. It is *not* a history of twentieth-century American social theory. It is *not* a compendium of Blumer's publications.

What it *is* is simply an attempt to break with narrowly historical readings in order to view Blumer's methodology in its methodological significance.

Note

1 This is the view Blumer has gone on record as favoring. In a brief exchange in 1967 with Joseph Woelfel, the question of proper interpretation arose for the specific case of how Mead was to be read. Woelfel argued that Mead's thought needs to be constructed rather than merely reproduced:

> Perhaps we should be less concerned with 'getting it right,' with finding out what Mead 'really said,' and pay more attention to what he could have said and should have said using the concepts he developed, or something like them (Woelfel, 1967: 409).

Blumer responded that Woelfel was "uttering nonsense" in claiming that "it makes no sense at all to discover what Mead 'really said' or 'really meant' " (Blumer, 1967b: 411):

I am definitely concerned with what Mead *said* and *meant*. The task here is not that of trying to unearth some 'intrinsic nature' or 'inner essence' of Mead's scheme of thought . . . but, instead, that of trying to determine what kind of object his scheme of thought was to Mead himself. This is what we always do whenever we seek to find out what a person meant in the disclosure of his thought (1967b: 411).

Blumer goes on to suggest that Woelfel's view implies a thoroughgoing interpretive relativism wherein "any version by any commentator . . . qualifies as a depiction." The end result is "scholarship at its lowest level" (1967b: 411).

The debate between Woelfel and Blumer involves some much disputed issues in the theory of interpretation. As is evident in the "Preface," the position upon which this study is based is closer to Woelfel's side of the argument than to Blumer's. For a critical treatment of Blumer's position on interpretation, see Chapter 4, especially "Blumer versus Erving Goffman."

1. What is methodology?

Like many other technical and quasi-technical terms in the social sciences, the word "methodology" has no single, uniform meaning. We must begin therefore with an attempt to become clear about Blumer's definition of it.

For Blumer, the methodology of science, in its most general expression, is the self-reflection of the scientific enterprise, that is, the study of the principles which underlie scientific inquiry (1969b: 24). This definition implies that, as with every self-reflective endeavor, methodology has an indefinite boundary. Its further reaches pass into the philosophical provinces of logic, epistemology, and ontology, blending fully into the array of their discourses. For this reason, Blumer's statement defining methodology begins with a discussion of idealism and realism (1969b: 21–2).

On the other hand, methodology is at least provisionally sited in a more familiar place. As the self-reflection of scientific inquiry, methodology is directed to recognize that inquiry in its entirety. From standard practice, Blumer gleans some key elements which fall into the proper focus of methodology: establishing a perspective for viewing the empirical world, raising research problems within that perspective, deciding on appropriate data and the methods for their collection, and prefiguring a framework for interpreting the findings of research (1969b: 26). Methodology addresses these matters not by enacting them, but by developing the *principles* according to which they are enacted.

We can grasp the full significance of Blumer's definition of methodology by considering how he employs it polemically. Throughout his career, Blumer was an outspoken critic of all attempts in sociology to narrow the domain of methodological discussion to an exclusive concern with methods or techniques. In his very first published paper, he stated:

I suspect that the milling and halting condition of our own science does not come directly from the inadequacy of our techniques, as almost everyone contends, but from the inadequacy of our point of view. The effort to rescue the discipline by

1

increasing occupation with method and by the introduction of precision devices is, I venture to suggest, working along the wrong direction (1931: 528).

Speaking before the American Sociological Society in 1947, Blumer upbraided certain of his colleagues:

I believe it is fair to say that those trying to study public opinion are so wedded to their technique that they shunt aside the vital question of whether their technique is suited to the study of what they are ostensibly seeking to study. Their work is largely merely making application of their technique (1948: 542).

More than two decades later, Blumer commented critically upon the "depressing frequency" with which methodology in the social sciences is equated with the study of quantitative procedures (1969b: 24). Aside from direct pronouncements, Blumer in his own methodological writings attempted to exemplify the proper scope of the discussion.

At issue in Blumer's critical stance is the role of reflection in science. Blumer insists that social science must be reflectively engaged with itself, for otherwise it will perpetuate several serious shortcomings, which we can recount in three steps.

First, Blumer considers the position of those who would simply truncate methodology into method (1966c: iii–vi). Their belief is that the essential character and principles of scientific practice are already established. With these principles as given, the task narrows to one of application, which is essentially a technical problem of translating scientific method into specific procedures:

This focusing of interest and effort on the innovation and perfection of techniques signifies that, in the study of man, no special problem is seen other than to work out appropriate applications of the scientific method. It is for this reason that the interest in 'methodology' in the social sciences is so predominantly preoccupied with the development and use of techniques (1966c: iv).

The point here is that technical considerations rely upon methodological principles in an implicit and naive fashion. To thematize these principles and assess them critically is nothing other than the self-reflection of scientific inquiry. Blumer's insistence upon the necessity of this task is an admonition for social science to grasp itself more critically.

The second concern underlying Blumer's defense of self-reflective social science involves rejection of a general view frequently interwoven with methodological principles implicitly employed. That view holds scientific method to be an established given. Proponents of this opinion frequently assume without further question that the physical sciences constitute a clear paradigm for all scientificity.

Yet a close look at the methodological thinking of the physical sciences, Blumer argues, reveals "an arena of difference, ambiguity, confusion, and, indeed, controversy." The conceptions of science in the natural sciences "do not reflect in any sense a unitary and firmly established view. Instead, they show significant differences along many lines" (1966c: iv). In sum, there is just "no consensus as to what constitutes 'scientific method'" (1966c: v).

We are too easily misled, Blumer continues, by the appearance from time to time of a seeming consensus. To avoid deception we must view such matters in a less parochial context:

The history of the portrayals of scientific method over the past two centuries by natural scientists and sophisticated interpreters shows a . . . picture of differences, change, shifts, and new versions. The nature of scientific method has not been, and is not now, a fixed, established datum (1966c: v).

Blumer's position poses the challenge of new beginnings. When in 1966 he declared flatly that the most important problem facing the social and psychological sciences is the question of how to study man (1966c: vi), he resumed the problematic that had engaged the founding fathers of the social sciences. For Durkheim, for Max Weber, for Simmel, methodology implied the need for broad-based reflection. These theorists, and of course many others, faced the challenge of inventing a discipline, and could not evade the fundament of such a task. What Blumer is urging is that we, too, remain beginners, and only deceive ourselves in thinking otherwise.

The third and last concern motivating Blumer's insistence upon a reflective social science involves *specific* methodological principles that are implicitly relied upon. Blumer argues in effect that, although methodology is not established as a fixed datum, it is still developed to the point where it can raise serious objections to certain uncritically employed procedures and techniques in social science. As we will see in the following chapters, Blumer's specific criticisms extend in several directions and occur on different levels of reflection. But for now, because we are considering methodology only in its most general aspect, let it simply be stated that, in Blumer's view, social science needs to reflect on its methods and practices in order to correct some current mistakes.

Such, then, is Blumer's case for self-reflection in social science. His argument is not an attack upon technical competence, but only upon the naiveté, sclerotic dogmatism, and error which can ensue when reflection is plied too narrowly.

It is important to recognize that Blumer's notion of methodology has no initial leanings toward qualitative, or ethnographic, research. Typically, Blumer is viewed in methodological terms as simply a theorist of participant observation. This error apparently draws from two sources. First, in his statement defining methodology (1969b: 21ff.), Blumer does not disengage as thoroughly as he might the definition of the term from its specific implementation. Second, many readers consider only the 1969 paper, "The methodological position of symbolic interactionism," and neglect the earlier writings. These two tendencies in fact converge: The failure to consider the earlier writings, which differ with the 1969 paper in significant ways, facilitates the analytic blurring of "methodology" with its more narrow implications. In consequence, Blumer is situated wrongly.

We need to center the matter. Blumer's view of methodology as the self-reflection of scientific inquiry implies a *general* problematic. And such is the outcome. Blumer grapples with issues which are logically prior to the distinction between quantitative and qualitative research. Any special attention devoted to the latter is derivative from considerations of a more fundamental nature. Blumer's message is for all social scientists, not just a coterie of ethnographers.

Having grasped the presiding thought in Blumer's conception of methodology, we may proceed to the more arduous task of following his implementation of it. In short, we must examine the results of Blumer's reflection on science, a reflection which bears a certain variegated quality.

For Blumer's thinking is not of a single piece. Having spanned half a century, it underwent change and development, a fact virtually lost to the Blumer secondary literature. Let us correct matters by proceeding, in the next chapter, to depict Blumer's methodological thought in its stages of development.

2. Blumer's development

First phase: Science and interpretation

The first phase of Blumer's development is dominated by two distinct tendencies. On the one hand, Blumer sought to uphold the methodological unity of the sciences. "*A priori,*" he said in his doctoral dissertation, "there is nothing in human behavior which prevents the application of the natural scientific method to human behavior" (1928: 32). Yet, one facet of the human studies did indeed trouble Blumer's quest for methodological unity, and that facet was interpretive understanding. Blumer granted the substantive importance of such understanding even as he recognized some difficulties it posed for his view of proper scientific procedure. In consequence, Blumer's first phase is constantly thwarted by a *tensional treatment of science and interpretation*. We will follow this tension through its course in Blumer's earliest writings.

Initial bearings: The dissertation. The doctoral dissertation, *Method in Social Psychology* (1928), opens Blumer's first phase of methodological reflection. The work comprises four chapters. In the first (1928: 1–53), Blumer considers the nature of scientific method as well as some other approaches which had been suggested in light of the putatively special features of human behavior. In the second chapter (1928: 54–246), Blumer attempts to delineate the field of social psychology by critically reviewing how a number of authors had construed it. The third chapter (1928: 247–406), which attempts to align the first two, turns to the methods employed by social psychology to examine them "mainly with respect to their prejudgments" (1928: 249), that is, their orienting theoretical perspectives. The final chapter looks briefly at the "data and devices" of social psychology.

It is the first chapter, then, where we gather Blumer's view of science. He distinguishes three aspects of scientific procedure: the functional, the logical, and the technical (1928: 2–27). In its functional aspect, science aims to simplify perceptual reality by the isolation, conceptualization, and ongoing reconstruction of universal instrumental relations. Blumer elaborates on this aim as follows. The world per se, he notes, is too complex for any "photographic representation;" it is capable of endless combination and division, alternately continuous and heterogeneous, and thus requires a *simplified transformation* in order for knowledge to be possible (1928: 3).

Furthermore, scientific inquiry requires the simplification of experience such that an instrumental relation between objects can be isolated. By "instrumental relation" Blumer means simply that one factor indicates another; ". . . scientific procedure aims at the isolation of a relation between two or more variables" (1928: 6–7). In regard to the objects so isolated, Blumer tells us that they must be durable and repetitive, accessible to others, and transmissible by discourse; in other words, they must be objective (1928: 6).

The most important feature of the relationships isolated by science is their universal character, their permitting no exceptions (1928: 9). Indeed, it is the exception which motivates reconstruction of the universal. How this occurs leads us to the next aspect of scientific procedure, its logical phase.

Blumer acknowledges that there are well-defined logical processes involved in scientific procedure – processes such as induction, deduction, classification, and framing hypotheses – but he denies that these actually occur in any straightforward sequence (1928: 13). In any case, *some* sense of sequence is roughly suggested in the following. Scientific inquiry begins with a problem, that is, with certain phenomena to which the prevailing fund of universal meanings is unable to apply (1928: 14). This motivates a number of activities which accompany and interpenetrate each other: observation, induction, classification, deduction, the framing of hypotheses and experimentation.

In regard to induction, Blumer cautions against viewing it as *the* constituent of true science, since induction leads merely to a "photographic representation" of reality. "What science requires, however, is a transformation of reality into an intelligible and comprehensible picture," which, in turn, "requires a deductive approach – that is, some scheme of selecting facts" (1928: 16). Instances of interest to science need to be "chosen because of their connection to some conception of the investigator" (1928: 16).

Such a conception is crystallized in the hypothesis, which is a proposed reconstruction of the universal in the face of exceptional instances. The hypothesis, along with experimentation, is a cornerstone of science (1928:

10); the two, indeed, require each other: "Experimentation should always accompany the framing of hypotheses" (1928: 22). The value of experimentation lies in its character as a closed system – that is, its elimination of irrelevant matters – and thus its facilitating the isolation of functional relationships.

The third aspect of scientific inquiry, its technical character, refers to the particular techniques and methods employed; these Blumer sees as varying from science to science (1928: 24) and hence as requiring no specification in the general consideration of science per se.

Having indicated the generic features of science, Blumer confronts the problems faced by interpretive understanding when it is assessed in light of those features. This discussion occurs in his consideration of sympathetic introspection (1928: 37ff., 335–42). That notion, borrowed from C. H. Cooley though adapted by Blumer, refers to the self-identification of the observer with the observed (1928: 335). Since Blumer wished to avoid Cooley's subjectivism (cf. 1928: 336), he adapted the technique such that self-identification came to be conceived as placing action inside of an act (1928: 336). Still, the procedure held numerous methodological deficiencies, which Blumer did not hesitate to underscore (1928: 41, 341ff.).

Even with its admitted drawbacks, however, Blumer found sympathetic introspection to be indispensable to social inquiry, for only with that method could social phenomena be understood in their full significance (1928: 343). "The method of sympathetic introspection is . . . indeed necessary – whatever be its shortcomings" (1928: 344). Blumer thus firmly planted a tension between science and interpretation without posing any means by which it could be resolved.

He did proceed to clarify the tension. Given the necessity of sympathetic introspection – that is, the comprehension of particular phenomena in their uniqueness – the question arose whether the generalizations sought by science could be extracted from the study of individual cases. Blumer's conclusion was pessimistic (cf. 1928: 364); he noted several matters which seemed to preclude generalizing from single cases.

First, rendering the single case intelligible depends upon the judgment, purpose, and values of the investigator (1928: 352), with the consequence that the items interpreted do not appear to have the stability which is so essential to classification and comparison in the natural sciences (1928: 353). The success of natural scientific classification, Blumer tells us, depends upon the "presence of fixed characters in the objects or instances to be classified" (1928: 353). Second, the instances of interpretive attention are normally of a complex character (1928: 354), whereas a guiding principle in science is to shun complexity and "seek to secure as simple a situation as possible" (1928: 358). Social science, generally, had failed to develop appropriate simplification techniques (1928: 378–9), and hence faced a definite predicament in its quest for generalized knowledge:

It would seem that investigation which aimed at the isolation of 'universals' such as characterize natural science would have to rely solely upon the classification of the unique or complex. However dismal this may leave the picture with respect to the possibility of introducing a natural scientific technique in social psychology, it is at least worthwhile to realize that this is the situation (1928: 391).

Exacerbating this "dismal picture" was Blumer's insistence upon the integral bond between theoretical orientation and research methods such that one implies the other. This feature, which I shall term *methodical holism,* constitutes (along with the unity of science theme) a basic structuring issue of Blumer's dissertation. Blumer utilizes his distinction between the functional, the logical, and the technical aspects of science to characterize both the unity of science and methodical holism. In this regard, he wrote:

One should see that the common features of procedure in different sciences are constituted by the functional and logical elements – also that the distinguishing marks belong to the technical aspects (1928: 27).

Thus, holism was held to apply only to the technical facet of science, though here Blumer was quite emphatic as to its importance: ". . . *scientific procedure in a given field must employ techniques adaptable to its particular problems*" (1928: 27), which is to say that it must not allow its subject matter to be "squeezed to fit into an *a priori* conceived technique" (1928: 258).

Blumer wants to confine the bond between theory and method to the technical aspect of science while *simultaneously* employing as normative criteria the functional and logical requirements of science per se. What happens is that methodical holism is constantly threatening to burst its containment, to press the methodical claims which follow from a theoretical recognition of meaningful speech and action beyond what is allowed by Blumer's conception of proper science. Although Blumer does not relent in assigning supremacy to the unity of science, he recognizes that such unity is more a hope than an actuality.

Science and action.   In his first published paper, "Science without concepts" (1931), Blumer temporarily set aside his doubts about the scientific legitimacy of interpretation in order to pursue untroubled the unity of science theme. He addresses a certain ambivalence: on the one hand, a recognition of the inevitability of concepts in science, and, on the other, a suspicion that those very concepts lure scientists into metaphysics. Blumer seeks to determine what truth underlies this ambivalence by identifying both the proper uses and the abuses of concepts in science. He proceeds by examining their function, disclaiming any interest in their epistemological properties (1931: 517).

Pragmatist psychology provides Blumer's point of departure. According to that psychology, perception and conception operate in an ongoing interchange. Perception itself results from the interplay of an organism's activity and its environment (1931: 517). That is, perception is not merely the passive reception of a world "out there," but is rather the selectively sensitized attending to such an environment induced by the action-related dispositional states of the organism.

As long as action continues in a "smooth flow," perception is instrumentally sufficient. When action is interrupted, blocked, or otherwise frustrated, however, perception may become insufficient, and a conceptual process is motivated. Conception reorganizes perception, offers up new objects and new possibilities of action. A concept is a tool that, if successful, facilitates a restoration of activity through surmounting the problem which had previously blocked it.

Blumer provides an episode from the history of biology to demonstrate the applicability of pragmatist psychology for elucidating scientific inquiry (1931: 519–20). Anthrax had for centuries proved to be a recalcitrant problem. When scientists came to study it, their initial efforts were stymied; perception of the disease remained puzzling and problematic. They did recognize that in the blood of stricken cattle there were small, rod-like organisms called "vibriones," but the significance of these organisms was not grasped.

It remained for Pasteur to approach the problem with a new concept, that of the infinitely small. With this notion he was able to develop novel experiments, to demonstrate the significance of "vibriones," and eventually to provide a solution to the problem of anthrax which resulted in its effective control. This episode, says Blumer, illustrates how the concept arises in response to problems, how it reorganizes and guides perception, and how it liberates blocked action by opening up new directions for proceeding.

So far the concept has been considered as a functional component of acting. But concepts also have another aspect, namely, a content conceived. In schematic form, Blumer's position in regard to this second aspect appears to be the following: The perceptual world is one of particulars; although it always involves conception, the latter operates through particulars (1931: 520). The concept, by comparison, is an abstraction (1931: 520); it is a class term, a universal.

Semantically considered, at least some concepts have a referent which is not directly perceived (1931: 518); scientific notions such as mass, motion, electricity, atom, culture, gene, heredity, etc., are examples here. Not only do we presume the existence of the nonperceived referents of these concepts, but we also suppose the referents to have a nature or a certain character (1931: 519). This character is conveyed in the connotation of the concept (cf. 1931: 523), which arises in reflection (1931: 518) and can be elaborated deductively (1931: 529). The semantic connection of concept with percept lies in the requirement that at least some terms in a conceptual framework receive partial interpretation through incorporating predicates which name aspects of what is given to perception as a series of particulars. Thus, conception can be said to reorganize perception (1931: 527), introducing new configurations of meaning, through the semantic re-synthesis of observable and nonobservable predicates.

The concept has a verbal or symbolic character that permits it to become an item of social discourse; thus, its content can become common property (1931: 522). Scientific concepts, according to Blumer, always originate in the experience of an individual (1931: 522). By passing into common possession, they enable collective action, the concerted organization of scientific inquiry (1931: 522).

Blumer goes on to distinguish between the concepts of science and those of commonsense (1931: 522–5). Commonsense concepts remain mired in the particularism of sense experience; they are apprehended vaguely, by denotation. The concepts of science, by comparison, are studied and analyzed in regard to their connotation; as Blumer would put it, their abstraction is pushed (1931: 523). In that process, conception acts back upon perception to open up new domains of evidence, which in turn may require revision of the concept. Commonsense concepts, by contrast, tend to remain static, their meanings unchanged. Lastly, the concepts of science, unlike those of common sense, tend to be organized and linked together systematically in coherent frameworks.

Having considered the functions of concepts and distinguished between scientific and commonsense concepts, Blumer concludes his paper by identifying four ways in which concepts are abused in science (1931: 503–533). The first manner of abuse lies in removing concepts from the world of experience and constructing their meanings without the constraint of empirical testing. In this way, concepts become, Blumer argues, "mere gossamer" (1931: 531). The second style of abuse consists in the reckless manufacture of concepts with no attention to whether they are needed. The third lies in the belief that to label something with a concept is to explain it, thereby terminating inquiry. On the contrary, Blumer insists, a concept is just a beginning, an instrument to be acted upon and revised as needed. The fourth abuse of concepts consists in treating scientific concepts in a commonsense fashion, that is, in sensing loosely, rather than comprehending clearly, their meanings.

In summary, we can see that in his first paper Blumer offers a general and selective sketch, rather than a close analysis, of scientific inquiry. According to that sketch, science is a form of action which systematically strives to achieve understanding and control (1931: 532) over a natural environment which offers resistance to such efforts. To overcome the resistance, science devises conceptual schemes which recast experience of the world, therewith reordering action. The continuation of action is synonymous with the success of science.

But here we must pause to consider the matter more closely. What Blumer has attempted to do – and in this his early work is characteristic of his life-long methodological thinking – is to conduct the self-reflection of science as its self-criticism. His intent, that is, is normative. Through reflection, Blumer arrives at his basic normative principle, which is that "the success of the activity to which it gives rise becomes the test of the effectiveness of the concept" (1931:528). This principle serves as the basis for demarcating science from metaphysics (1931: 531) as well as the standard by which scientific concepts are judged. In brief, Blumer treats the "success criterion" as *sufficient* for characterizing the normative methodological framework of science.

But this overburdens the capabilities of that criterion with demands it cannot meet. To speak of "liberating blocked action" is vague and general; it is not at all clear how any concept can be rejected on the basis of that principle, since in some fashion or other, any concept can "free action" insofar as that notion is not defined in a specific sense that would differentiate some concepts from others. The conclusion which follows is that Blumer's first published effort is left floundering in its own vagueness. Of course, when viewed within the context of the dissertation, where he had introduced a number of *necessary* conditions for scientific procedure, the argument in "Science without concepts" can be specified more clearly: The functional aspect of science, in particular, can be regarded as providing the conditions which make possible any successful continuation of blocked action, the latter conceived as instrumental control over objectified processes. But Blumer never expressly draws this connection. As it stands, then, Blumer's paper is truncated and untenable.

In none of his methodological writings subsequent to "Science without concepts" does Blumer treat the "success criterion" as *sufficient* for depicting the normative basis of scientific inquiry. Whether he viewed the criterion as *necessary* for depicting that basis is doubtful. Writing in 1939, Blumer again emphasized his instrumentality thesis: "The ultimate test of the validity of scientific knowledge is the ability to use it for purposes of social control" (1939: 70; also 115). Yet, as his thinking developed, the "success criterion" faded from view. It is reasonable to conjecture that the fading of the criterion corresponds with the fading of the unity of science theme in Blumer's methodology – with the transition beyond his first phase of development.

In 1931, however, and indeed for several more years, that unity remained paramount, at least in aspiration. Of special note is the fact that the chief illustrative examples in "Science without concepts" are taken from *natural* science. Yet try as he might, Blumer could never forget interpretation nor accommodate it within his early methodological framework. We turn now to witness the return of this temporarily suppressed tension.

Symbolic interactionism versus behaviorism.   In 1937, Blumer contributed a chapter to a volume entitled *Man and Society*. That chapter, called simply "Social psychology," provides an overview of the discipline with some important methodological implications.

Blumer identifies as the two most important theoretical orientations in social psychology the stimulus–response approach and symbolic interactionism (1937a: 187). For purposes of research these different orientations exert a crucial bearing, since, according to the thesis of methodical holism, "different points of view dictate what kind of problems are to be selected for study, and what methods are to be employed in the investigation" (1937a: 187). Blumer goes on to specify this thesis for the two orientations he has singled out.

The stimulus–response orientation focuses attention upon limited units of conduct, that is, those which can be subsumed under the stimulus–response couplet. In order to detect such behavior, researchers must establish conditions in which it can be isolated and controlled: laboratory conditions. Alternately, the stimulus–response orientation favors the use of investigatory devices such as questionnaires, schedules, and tests, where the given items function seemingly as stimuli and the replies as responses. Generally, since it is fundamentally a neurological scheme, the stimulus–response orientation permits – even requires – research to focus upon observable behaviors, and thus to secure "objective" data. Given such data, quantitative analytic procedures are facilitated.

The symbolic interactionist orientation implies a rather different line of research. Theoretically, the interactionist approach identifies as its basic unit *action;* the stimulus–response scheme, by contrast, directs attention to *reaction.* The difference between the two is not merely verbal. For the interactionist, activity "begins with an inner impulse rather than with an external stimulus" (1937a: 192); this impulse, which is tantamount to tension and discomfort, impels the organism to act. Typically, the impulse calls up images which offer some means for its satisfaction; in turn, the images give rise to a goal or objective. The latter may be immediate or remote; it may undergo an extensive career even before it gains any behavioral expression. Such a career may consist of a "very elaborate and rich inner development" (1937a: 193), a transformative process in which the final behavioral form of the act is constituted. Given the constructive significance of this inner process, the external phase of the act, central to the stimulus–response approach, dims in comparative significance.

The foregoing theoretical considerations direct research to the area of inner experience. Methodically, this research would employ such devices as the life history, the interview, the autobiography, the case method, diaries, and letters (1937a: 194). With these tools, research is able to grasp the experience of persons and hence to make intelligible their behavior.

Having stated the unity of theory and method for the respective positions of stimulus–response psychology and symbolic interactionism, Blumer describes the debate that rages between the two perspectives. From their side the interactionists accuse the stimulus–response partisans of ignoring what is most essential to human behavior, its symbolic–constructive aspect. Without that aspect, their argument goes, no social psychology can hope to provide an accurate depiction of its subject matter.

The stimulus–response psychologists rejoin that research initiated under the auspices of symbolic interactionism is hardly scientific at all. Scientific knowledge requires data that are precise, open to public validation, comparable for purposes of generalization, and amenable to quantitative treatment. Interactionist research, it is alleged, does not meet these requirements and hence cannot be pursued as science.

"So far," Blumer concludes the discussion, "the basic issue between these two divergent approaches has not been settled, nor have the differences been reconciled" (1937a: 196). This admission is highly instructive when we reflect further upon the character of the debate. The symbolic interactionists base their criticism of the stimulus–response approach on considerations as to the nature of that which is the object of their research. The stimulus–response psychologists, on the other hand, criticize the interactionist perspective on methodological grounds, alleging that it does not employ the appropriate procedures of science. The debate thus hinges on the relative importance assigned to substantive orientation or to method: For the interactionists, it is the former which takes precedence, whereas for the stimulus–response psychologists, it is the latter. The controversy is compounded by the fact that the theoretically implied methods of interactionism are not those which the stimulus–response partisans regard as genuinely scientific. The fact that Blumer describes the debate as unsettled attests to the unresolved tension in his own methodological reflection between the claims of science and the need to grasp the social world through the process of interpretive understanding.

The dilemma of verification. In 1939, two years after "Social psychology", Blumer published a critical review of Thomas and Znaniecki's *The Polish Peasant in Europe and America.* Included in the publication is the transcript of a conference, held late in 1938, during which Blumer's review was discussed by a group of social scientists, including such notables as Gordon Allport, Samuel Stouffer, W. I. Thomas, Louis Wirth, and Blumer himself. Since both Blumer's review and his contributions to the conference are highly illuminating of his methodological thinking at the time, we will consider both.

In his examination of *The Polish Peasant,* Blumer begins by attempting to pare that massive tome down to its methodological essentials. This effort is very much in the spirit of the work itself, whose avowed purpose is the explication and exemplification of a standpoint and method (1939: 6). The latter consists in a number of principles which we can briefly recount.

First, Thomas and Znaniecki insist upon the need for a scheme of research geared to a society undergoing change and transition. Second, the authors insist that the study of human social life requires recognition of both objective and subjective factors; they designate these, respectively, values and attitudes, terms which serve as their most basic theoretical units. Third, Thomas and Znaniecki intend to establish lawlike causal relations between the factors that are involved in social change, that is, casual relations between values and attitudes, and vice versa. Fourth, in order to establish laws, Thomas and Znaniecki stress three procedures:

the use of a comparative method involving scrutiny of many instances of a given attitude and value to determine the relation between them; the interpretation of attitudes and values within the context of the whole of social life; and, when generalizations are proposed, the systematic search for negative examples. Fifth, Thomas and Znaniecki view the outcome of their research as practical application for the purpose of social control. Sixth, given their recognition of the subjective factor in human life, Thomas and Znaniecki have indicated a need for a certain type of data, and they obtain these data through the use of "human documents," or records of human experiences.

Blumer reacts to the above delineated methodological scheme with a number of critical considerations. He notes that the basic theoretical terms – "attitudes" and "values" – are vague and confused (1939: 25). Definitions of the terms tend to identify rather than demarcate them; hence, a logical difficulty arises in treating them as separate entities that are causally related. Further, the question of how values operate on attitudes raises another vexing issue: Since, for Thomas and Znaniecki, the relation between the two terms is mediated by a varying definition of the situation, this mediation would tend to undermine the search for invariant causal laws. The fact that Thomas and Znaniecki did not establish any "laws of social becoming," nor did they even propose many, attests, Blumer argues, to the logical flaws of their basic methodological formula. On the other hand, considered very generally, the formula, which accords subjective factors a role of importance for social life, "seems distinctly valid" (1939: 28).

The use made by Thomas and Znaniecki of human documents invites another critical response by Blumer. According to the authors' express methodological requirement, documents need to be construed according to social context. Yet the letters used by Thomas and Znaniecki are not construed in this manner (1939: 35). Moreover, all of the documentary materials raise questions, to a greater or lesser degree, regarding their representativeness, adequacy, and reliability.

So far we have dealt with criticisms which, though important, do not reach the heart of the matter. Blumer's major topic for critical reflection concerns the relationship between theory and documentary evidence, a topic which, when generalized, becomes nothing less than the question of what constitutes theory verification. Yet, it is just this generalized issue with which Blumer, at least in 1938, is demonstrably uncomfortable. When queried about the criteria for validating theory, he responded, "You raise a question which I do not feel competent to answer" (1939:

112). Later, he added, "I do not want to be led into a discussion of criteria of validity" (1939: 115). Nonetheless, Blumer could not avoid such discussion, since he had already broached it in his critical assessment of the relationship between theory and documentary evidence in *The Polish Peasant*. As we proceed to examine Blumer's view of theory verification, we will see that his thinking was altogether tentative, consisting only of an assortment of unconsolidated hunches and tendencies. We can arrive at the first of these tendencies by following out his critique of Thomas and Znaniecki.

Blumer notes immediately that for the two authors theory was not derived inductively from the data. The major theoretical schemes were already adumbrated in the writings of Thomas; even the particular interpretations were at least partly imported. "Thus," Blumer concludes:

while there can be no question but that much of the theoretical conception of the authors came from handling the documents, it is also true that a large part of it did not (1939: 74).

But no matter. The important question is whether the data adequately test the theory. Blumer answers that, generally, they do not (1939: 75). Although he does not explicate his understanding of theory testing, we can infer some of its features by considering why he believes that documentary material fails for testing purposes.

The failure stems from the peculiar nature of the relationship between theory and the evidence, a relationship Blumer gropes to describe (1939: 38). On the one hand, it is apparent that the letters used by Thomas and Znaniecki are not the source from which their theory is inductively derived. Yet, on the other hand, the letters do more than merely illustrate the theory. "The actual relation is somewhere in between" (1939: 38). It is clear that Thomas and Znaniecki did derive many theoretical insights from the letters, and also clear that their prior theoretical commitments "guided and frequently coerced their interpretations of the letters" (1939:38). The interaction between theory and evidence, as Blumer sees it, is thus "exceedingly ambiguous" (1939: 38).

We might remove the ambiguity by recognizing it to be a semantic reciprocity holding between theory and documentary evidence. On one side, theory projects new determinations upon the evidence; this is especially so in regard to "abstract interpretations." "Simple facts," by contrast, do allow for disproof on the basis of documentary evidence (1939: 77). It is the abstract interpretations, then, which pose a difficulty for verification, a difficulty that Blumer perceives in the ease with which documents lend themselves to diverse interpretations. "Theories seem to order the data" (1939: 77).

It is this last feature which, to Blumer, annuls any possibility for data to test theory. Why, then, is theory able to order the data? The answer to this question is decisive, since for Blumer it provides possible remedial steps that can be taken to allow for proper theory testing. We need to follow his answer with some care.

In the first place, it is only abstract theoretical principles which exert an ordering effect upon the data. But, Blumer argues, it is not the abstractness per se which is responsible; instead, he identifies another culprit. Interpretation involves the application of concepts or categories, and, with human documents, it frequently seems that any concepts congenial to the interpreter can be made to fit:

Part of the difficulty comes from the fact that the categories employed are left undefined, or else are defined in an imprecise manner. Consequently, one is at a loss to identify details of experience that would permit one to determine whether or not the category fits. The application of the category is a matter of judicious judgment rather than decisive test (1939: 78).

Blumer has made some crucial connections in this passage. The chief reason that abstract concepts can order data is that concepts are undefined or defined only vaguely, and this in turn means that they are removed from experiential referents. The lesson he draws is that concepts need to be grounded empirically if their application is to be a "decisive test" rather than a matter of "judicious judgment."

On the basis of this lesson, we can piece together its implicit background, which turns out to be a rather facile model of theory testing. Blumer supposes a version of empiricism which is both syntactically and semantically reductive. It is syntactically reductive insofar as it takes as its unit of analysis the concept; it does not consider other formal configurations and how these specify further the requirements of theory testing. Blumer's empiricism is also semantically reductive in that it seeks to delimit scientific concepts to those defined on the basis of experiential predicates.

An example might clarify this view. Suppose one person points and says to another, "Look at the sparrow" and the second person, knowing the meaning of the word "sparrow," glances and establishes that the bird in the tree is in fact a sparrow. The second person is said to have tested and confirmed the statement. The model of theory testing behind Blumer's remarks appears to be nothing more than what this simple, and indeed simplistic, example serves to illustrate. We might label it a look-and-see empiricism.

Such a view departs significantly from Blumer's thinking in "Science without concepts." There he had presented a semantic analysis of concepts which was not reductive. Recall that concepts were said to have referents which are not directly perceived, and that the referents have a nature which arises in reflection and can be elaborated deductively. Moreover, though his discussion is somewhat diffuse, in the earlier work Blumer had allowed that theory can have a semantic input into experience (cf. 1931: 519).

In the 1939 review, Blumer has in effect criticized his own earlier position. There the semantic analysis of concepts had not borne any epistemological chores; those chores were alloted to the "success criterion." Now, however, the weight of responsibility has shifted, and Blumer adds some necessary conditions to his thinking on theory confirmation.

Reflecting further, Blumer comments that the relationship between theory and data in the natural sciences is different from the relationship between theory and the data of human documents (1939: 113–14). With the latter relationship, theory, especially on its abstract levels, does not seem to depend for its validity upon the use of particular accounts of human experience (1939: 113). In the natural sciences, by contrast, theory does appear to be tested by specific instances of particular facts. Given Blumer's aspiration at the time for a methodological unity of science, this departure of social science from the natural science model can only signal its second-class status.

The relationship between theory and documentary evidence leaves social science with something of a dilemma. On the one hand, "the study of social life seems to require the understanding of the factor of human experience" (1939: 79). Yet this experience is not identified in ways which permit strict empirical testing of its interpretation. On the contrary, such interpretation remains a mere "matter of judgment" (1939: 80). It should be added that Blumer's concern in this issue is directly tied to his own empirical research. His earliest work investigated the impact of movies (1933; Blumer and Hauser 1933), relying for its chief source of data on what he termed "motion picture autobiographies."

Deriving at least partially from the verification troubles of social science is its apparent inability to establish strict laws of human experience. Blumer confesses to a skepticism regarding the prospect for such laws, but he does hold out hope for a body of "very useful" knowledge that would comprise generalizations (1939: 149). The status Blumer is willing to accord social research is somewhat peculiar, lying somewhere between establishing scientific laws and providing literary illumination (1939: 143). On the other hand, he expresses the hope that this situation is only provisional (1939: 143), corrigible possibly through developing ways of catching human experience "in the way that is customary for usable data in ordinary scientific procedure in other fields" (1939: 111). With such data, social science could perhaps approach more closely the "precise cause and effect relationships which we regard as necessary for science" (1939: 142).

In the meantime, however, social science must rely on human documents for data. Why, then, cannot the predicament of theory confirmation be resolved on the basis of Blumer's recommendation for a semantically reductive treatment of theory terms? It is, after all, the abstract, ambiguous concepts which, according to Blumer, account for the problem in the first place. To replace these terms with others having a clear empirical referent would apparently eliminate the difficulty.

But Blumer has second thoughts about his reductive semantics. In the effort to apply theoretical interpretations to human experience, he tells us that "the more precise and unambiguous the terms, the less valuable they are" (1939: 124). The reason for this, as he sees it, is that when "vague and indefinite" concepts are broken down into terms that can be tested empirically, something appears to be lost; some aspect of the original cannot be reexpressed in a more definite translation (1939: 162).

Given these doubts about the viability of semantic reduction, the problem of testing theory with documentary evidence remains. If such evidence cannot provide a strict test of theory, how, then, is social theory to be tested? Reluctantly, Blumer suggests some other criteria: consistency with other theories regarded as tenable, self-consistency, applicability to broad rather than specific areas of human behavior, usefulness for making predictions, and, as the "ultimate test," the pragmatic criterion of controlling the data to which the theory refers (1939: 112, 115).

Since documentary data cannot test theory, what use is this evidence to social science? Blumer responds that documents have a heuristic value wherein they might yield, to the suitably attuned mind, hunches, insights, new perspectives, and new questions (1939: 76). In this way documents develop the judgment of those who study them. Blumer goes on to urge that intimate familiarity with the people being studied constitutes an expertise which warrants the deference of those who are not experts; such persons need to "temper their own judgments by some acceptance, on authority, of the analysis which the investigator makes of human documents" (1939: 81; cf. also 151).

Notice what Blumer has done in this appeal to the authority of the expert: He has shifted the discussion away from the criteria of theory verification to the fact of it. This shift was hinted at by one of the participants in the conference discussion: A judgment is not accepted because it comes from an "expert," but the latter is recognized as such when his or her judgment is evaluated and found to be solid (1939: 151). Thus, the real issue is that of the *grounds* for accepting or rejecting the judgment of the "expert." Blumer comes to admit this, though he is openly perplexed regarding just what constitutes the grounds of validation (1939: 152).

Blumer's earliest methodology, to sum it up, was an arena for battling tendencies: on one side, a desire for the methodological unity of the sciences, with natural science serving as paradigmatic for social inquiry, and, on the other side, a recognition that interpretive understanding, necessary for social inquiry, could not be accommodated within that unity. The conflict seemed to issue in stalemate. Further reflection clearly was motivated.

Second phase: The semantics of inquiry

Having reached an impasse in the conflicting claims of science and interpretation, Blumer set about to rethink his view of science. He picked up on his earlier suggestion for a look-and-see empiricism, founded on a reductive semantics, and proceeded to work toward a theoretical development of that position. The results, as we shall now gather, are far from satisfactory.

The troublesome concept. In 1940, Blumer published "The problem of the concept in social psychology." The paper begins with a critical recognition of the ambiguous and imprecise nature of concepts in social science. This state of affairs, Blumer argues, presents an obstruction to effective research, for it opens a gap between theory and empirical observation and, in addition, hinders rigorous deduction. What accounts for the gap between theory and observation is that theoretical concepts do not "indicate in any clear way the features of the thing to which the concept refers" (1940: 707). The consequence of the gap is that testing theory by observation is made difficult, speculation in the unfavorable sense of the term is facilitated, and, given the divergent directions taken by speculation, theoretical coherence is impeded.

Blumer argues that the bifurcation of conceptual usage and empirical investigation plagues social science generally, but in social psychology it constitutes the "major dilemma" of the field (1940: 709). There are, in effect, two separate and equally faulty directions taken in social psychology. In the first direction go those social psychologists who, repelled by conceptual vagueness and confusion, have opted for an atheoretical empiricism. Seeking exact data through the employment of precise techniques, they have flooded the discipline with a "plethora of censuses, tests, scales, scoring devices, and minor experiments" (1940: 708), all of which have done little to clarify concepts and hence little to advance theory.

In the other direction go those social psychologists who, theory-oriented, grapple with problems in a manner that should yield bona fide explanations. Yet the difficulty here, Blumer argues, is that proffered theoretical interpretations are "seldom subjected to rigorous test by empirical observation" (1940: 709). In part and in consequence, concepts remain vague.

The divergent directions in social psychology must be joined, Blumer urges, if the discipline is to acquire the character of a scientific endeavor (1940: 709). Such endeavor requires a working relationship wherein the facts of experience check theory, and theory organizes the facts of experience. This working relationship accounts for the achievements of natural science, and, indeed, defines science (1940: 709).

To bring together the divergent tendencies within social psychology requires an effort to eliminate the vagueness of concepts. A number of attempts in that direction have been made, and Blumer goes on to identify and criticize each of them.

The first proposal is to abandon prevailing concepts and develop new ones. The problem here, Blumer asserts, is that vagueness tends to reappear in the new concepts, a fact apparent when different psychological systems are compared (1940: 710). Moreover, there is a need for a new concept only where there is a new fact; otherwise, it is better to clarify time-held concepts, since, however vague, they are likely to denote something significant.[1]

The second proposal for eliminating ambiguity in concepts is the method of operational definition, which takes both a "moderate" and an "extreme" form. In the moderate form operationalism seeks to confine the meaning of a concept to quantitative data gathered with reference to it. Prevailing concepts, or some of them, are accepted and provided with a content through the implementation of certain measuring devices.

The problem with this form of operationalism, Blumer contends, is that it constitutes an unwarranted reductionism. It employs concepts which already have an established meaning and yet excises portions of that meaning which are not quantitatively determinable. In many cases what is omitted is the "most vital part of the original reference" (1940: 711). Unless it can be shown that the nonquantitative portions of a concept's meaning are dispensable, the moderate form of operationalism proves to be unworkable.

The other form of operationalism – its "extreme" version – disregards existing concepts and attempts to begin anew. Its procedure is to treat concepts as semantically exhausted by the results of some particular measuring device; for example, "intelligence" is what intelligence tests measure. The assumption is that a measurement device discloses some stable content, which in turn provides the meaning of the concept.

Blumer refers to extreme operationalism as an "interesting means of escaping the problem" (1940: 711). One central feature of this operationalism qualifies it as an escape: The operational definition has no nature, nothing generic that can be characterized and studied. Its stable content, if indeed it has such a thing, is but an unknowable X. Consequently, any significance that this X has comes about through quantified correlations with other unknowable symbols. The result would be "an exceedingly odd framework of interrelated symbols", which "would be nothing like concepts as we are familiar with them" (1940: 712).

We need such concepts in order to meet the demands of intelligibility and application. A set of unknowable symbols provides nothing generic; thinking requires generic concepts (i.e., universals). As a corollary, unknowable symbols run into problems whenever they come to be applied. To generate any applicability at all requires making recourse to generic concepts. For example, "intelligence" may be viewed as the numerical result of an intelligence test, but in order to apply the concept to actual human conduct, it must be viewed as standing for something generic, such as problem-solving ability. In this way the application of operationally defined concepts slips over into a concept of a different sort (1940: 712), indicating the inadequacy of the former. Extreme operationalism thus does not solve the problem of vague concepts; it merely displaces the problem.

The third proposal for eliminating the vagueness of concepts seeks to work from critical reflection, comparing different definitions and usages of a given term, eliminating inconsistencies, classifying related definitions, and thus establishing a precise definition which will allow for common usage of a concept (1940: 712–13). Blumer comments that this effort has value as a lexicographical exercise, but that it is not adequate to attack the problem of vague scientific concepts in its full scope. For that problem involves the empirical referents of concepts, and to treat the problem apart from such referents could easily exacerbate it, invoking all the negative connotations of the term "scholasticism."

So Blumer has considered, and rejected, some major ways of clarifying vague concepts. But instead of simply resolving the matter with his own recommendation, he sets about first to explicate more fully the conditions which make for conceptual vagueness. Since, for Blumer, the "vagueness of a concept is equivalent to a difficulty in observing clearly the thing to which the concept is presumed to refer" (1940: 713–14), he begins by considering the nature of observation, especially observation of human conduct.

One type of observation is that of physical action. Directly perceived and easily identified, such action occurs within a space–time framework where "people have common experience and therefore verifiable experience" (1940: 714). Given this verifiability, Blumer avers, observations of physical action tend not to give rise to dispute. It is this feature of effective validation which lends a certain appeal to behaviorism. If all human conduct could be treated as physical action, and if concepts were made to denote such action, then concepts in social psychology could be made precise with little difficulty.

But all human behavior cannot be reduced to physical action, Blumer continues. We commonly employ other types of observation to disclose human conduct in a different light. In one type of observation, a person is seen to act aggressively, respectfully, jealously, etc. Here the observation is founded upon a sense of the social relations involved in the occasion. For example, the characterization of an act as being respectful derives from viewing it from the perspective of rights and obligations operative within the setting (1940: 715).

Another sort of observation takes place when an act is viewed as intentional in character. Still another kind of observation occurs which freely goes beyond the field of visual perception; Blumer has in mind here the "observation" of written data, even of acts which have to be imagined (1940: 717).

Having indicated other types of observation besides that of physical action, Blumer probes into their character. What is clear is that observation involves inferences, and this is true even for observations of physical acts (1940: 715). Most frequently, the inference is fused immediately with the observation itself, making it inconspicuous. An inference becomes conspicuous where a situation is not immediately clear, and not only does it become conspicuous, but it also becomes less certain. In either case, the ". . . character that we observe in an act is lodged there through a process of inference" (1940: 715–16).

What does all this imply for the problem of vague concepts? Essentially, concepts are vague because the observations which serve them are "tenuous and uncertain," and observations have this character because of an "inability to form dependable judgments and inferences" (1940: 718). Moreover, at present, according to Blumer, undependable judgments and inferences are inherent to the kinds of observations which we necesarily must make and use (1940: 718).

But Blumer does not believe that the situation, difficult as it is, is totally hopeless. The remedy for vague concepts lies in securing dependable observation (1940: 718). This in turn depends upon "developing a rich and intimate familiarity with the kind of conduct that is being studied" and utilizing relevant imagination (1949: 719). With these steps, Blumer is assured, conceptual ambiguity can be gradually eliminated, though the process is bound to be slow and tedious.

"The problem of the concept in social psychology" is a difficult piece of writing made so in large part by a number of internal flaws. Indeed, from an analytic point of view, the argument is flawed beyond repair. To see this we need to work back through it with the critical intention of trying to sort out its claims and miscues.

What Blumer attempts to do in his 1940 paper is to make explicit the implications of theory testing as reductive semantics. Concepts denoting physical action can be "readily verified" (1940: 714) because physical action can be brought into a space–time framework which compels common experience on the part of observers (1940: 714). Given this common experience, founded by the world itself, effective validation of theory poses no difficulty.

Yet Blumer not only acknowledges the implications of reductive semantics, he recoils from them. For a strict adherence to that manner of theory testing would require for social science a wholesale conversion to behaviorism. Blumer wants none of that. Instead, he goes on to probe the nature of observation in such a way that serious problems arise for his look-and-see empiricism.

Basically, Blumer comes to recognize that the character of an observation is "lodged there through a process of inference" (1940: 715–16). This obviously is incompatible with the view put forth in the 1939 review, namely, that any semantic input from theory to data is prohibited. Yet Blumer continues to hold to the latter thesis, insisting that, whenever concepts "coerce the judgment and determine what is seen," "there can be no effective interaction between concept and empirical observation" (1940: 719). We might ask how concepts cannot in some sense determine what is seen since its character is lodged there on the basis of concepts. Having destroyed a central condition of his look-and-see empiricism, Blumer retains that perspective nonetheless.

We can see the shift in Blumer's thinking in another way. Originally, his problem concerned the validation of theoretical concepts on the basis of empirical observation. After having recognized that observation is inference-laden, Blumer turned to ponder the question of how *observation* can be validated (1940: 718). This shift in topical focus constitutes a problem that cannot be handled within the framework of the original model, for that model supposes observation to be semantically nonproblematic.

The gist of the matter is that Blumer's thinking unintentionally had shattered the very framework it sought to articulate. Yet Blumer did not fully apprehend this fact, as is evident in his handling of the question of how to secure dependable observation (1940: 718–19).

One way, he says, is to confine observation to physical action (1940: 718), since the space–time framework of such action compels common experience and thereby reliable observations. Yet Blumer apparently has forgotten that the basis for a common experience has been repudiated – "brute data" have turned out to be chimerical. As a result, common experience, compelled or otherwise, has become very problematic, not an automatic source of validational authority.

The second way we might obtain "dependable and verifiable" observations is to observe only the "simpler and easily detected kinds of social action" (1940: 718). This action makes for accurate observation because observers can readily grasp the social relations in which it is situated or else they can apprehend "dependable signs present in the behavior" (1940: 716). Given these conditions, in short, the inferences constituting observation become a common judgment reached by different observers.

Yet once again Blumer has neglected to admit the problematic character of common judgment. In his original model, it was the source of such judgment (i.e., "brute data"), and not the judgment itself, that made for reliability of observations. Now Blumer seems – quite unwittingly – to have slipped into conventionalism, a very different account of "theory testing" from that with which he began.

The third way of developing dependable observations does not involve any manner of narrowing the scope of what is observed; it admits the full and complex range of social psychological phenomena. This way requires "developing a rich and intimate familiarity with the kind of conduct that is being studied" and in the use of "relevant imagination" (1940: 719). Notice here that Blumer has abandoned the problem, which was to state how observation is to be made reliable; he says, in effect, that the way to achieve dependable observation is just to observe. But the qualification of observation by a normative consideration (dependable, reliable) implies the normative insufficiency of observation per se. And Blumer simply does not tell us what the normative basis is that he implicitly relies upon.

Apparently, Blumer wants to retain his original model for the 1940 paper (i.e., his look-and-see empiricism) despite the fact that his thinking has effectively refuted that model. On the other hand, there does seem to be some oblique awareness on Blumer's part of the real problems he has encountered. Appended to the text near the end is a note which indicates that, because of the inherent difficulty of observations and data in social psychology, it is unlikely that the discipline will be capable of validating its propositions in the effective manner of natural science. Instead, they will have to be appraised according to their reasonableness, their plausibility, and their illumination (1940: 719 fn.). In effect, Blumer has acknowledged some problems of his look-and-see model of theory testing, at least at a practical level.

It is important to note the change evident here over Blumer's position in the 1939 review. In the latter work he had provided some criteria for validating theory, urging as the "ultimate criterion" the instrumental use of theory for social control. Now he situates his look-and-see empiricism in center position and invokes other criteria when difficulties hinder implementation of that preferred criterion.

"The problem of the concept in social psychology" marks a shift and a development in Blumer's methodological thinking, yet not in a satisfactory direction. The paper is inconclusive, and Blumer, given the tentativeness of his formulations, seems to recognize this fact.

The rise and fall of the "sensitizing concept."   Fourteen years later, in 1954, Blumer returned to the "problem" of the concept in his paper, "What is wrong with social theory?" He begins the paper with a brief sketch of the role of theory in empirical science. Theory conceives the world abstractly, "in terms of classes of objects and of relations between such classes" (1954a: 3). Research follows up the implications of theory to see whether that are supported by the evidence. Theory thus influences research – "setting problems, staking out objects and leading inquiry into asserted relations" (1954a: 3) – and research in turn acts back upon theory to support or modify it. The interaction of theory, research, and fact constitutes the fruitful interplay through which an empirical science develops (1954a: 3).

Yet, compared to this ideal of procedure, social theory exhibits grave deficiencies in its relation to research (1954a: 3). Theory is held separate from empirical inquiry, existing in a closed and detached world of literature and exegesis. In part and in consequence, theory readily lies open to the "importation of schemes from outside its own empirical field," such as the organic analogy, behaviorism, psychoanalysis, etc. (1954a: 4). Furthermore, whenever social theory does broach empiricities, it does so not to be tested by them, but rather to press them into its mold (1954a: 4).

Another shortcoming of social theory is that it is "conspicuously defective in its guidance of research inquiry" (1954a: 4). Since it is rarely couched in testable forms, theory cannot fulfill its proper role of setting research problems, suggesting kinds of data to be sought, and adumbrating the manner in which these data are connected.

The third deficiency of social theory – actually a derivative of the first – is that it fails to accommodate the ever-growing body of research findings. These findings, abandoned by theory, are thus lost to intelligibility.

The deficiencies of social theory seem to suggest some ready guidelines for their own correction. Above all, get social theorists away from an exclusive exegetical concern with literature and back in touch with the empirical world. Require them to develop theories in response to that world instead of importing exogenous conceptual schemes. See that theory becomes tested by fact, which means that it must be couched in testable form. Finally, encourage theorists to digest the already gathered body of research findings.

These recommendations Blumer finds to have some merit, but to miss the essential point. For in fact a number of social theorists have followed these admonitions without apparent success. What remains to be done, Blumer argues, is to probe more deeply into the matter; only then, after identifying the most fundamental source of the deficiencies in social theory, will it be possible to consider remedies.

Blumer begins his analysis of the problem by identifying its locus. "In my judgment," he says, "the appropriate line of probing is with regard to the concept" (1954a: 4). And why is this so?

Theory is of value in empirical science only to the extent to which it connects fruitfully with the empirical world. Concepts are the means, and the only means of establishing such a connection, for it is the concept that points to the empirical instances about which a theoretical proposal is made (1954a: 4).

Immediately we see Blumer invoking his syntactic and semantic reductionism. The concept is his sole unit of analysis, and its meaning is treated by reference to what it denotes experientially. Thus, if a concept is clearly defined, we are able to identify what counts as an empirical instance of it; conversely, if a concept is vague, we cannot do so (1954a: 4–5). Without further question, Blumer equates conceptual vagueness with empirical ambiguity. That a concept might be clear and empirically ambiguous (or even nonempirical) does not occur to him; his semantic reductionism precludes it.

The root flaw of social theory, then, is conceptual vagueness. Typical terms such as "social institutions," "norms," "attitudes," "social structure," and so on "do not discriminate cleanly their empirical instances" (1954a: 5). In consequence, a gap is opened between theory and its empirical world, and with this gap arise all the deficiencies of social theory that Blumer has cataloged.

To resolve the problem requires a procedure for making concepts clear and definite. The only question is the nature of such a procedure. A number of would-be approaches do not even touch the problem; Blumer cites specifically the introduction of a new theoretical vocabulary or of new theories, logical analysis of theories, the invention of new technical instruments, the improvement of the reliability of old instruments, the compilation of research findings, and the extension in the scope and direction of research (1954a: 5–6).

The most serious attempts to correct conceptual vagueness have employed a procedure that "is designed to yield through repeated performances a stable and definitive finding" (1954a: 6). This procedure can be implemented through a number of different technical maneuvers, such as the use of operational definitions, factor analysis, the construction of deductive mathematical systems or reliable quantitative indexes, and the experimental construction of concepts (1954a: 6). Blumer does not attend to the differential merit (or demerit) of these various technical maneuvers; instead, he criticizes them generically through what he sees as their common denominator: the attempt to arrive at conceptual content through blind empirical groping.

Against such groping Blumer for the most part simply repeats the criticism of operational definitions offered in his 1940 paper. Such definitions are not genuine concepts because they are not universals having specifiable attributes. Moreover, any attempt to give them a specifiable character reintroduces concepts of a nonoperational kind, and thus the problem of conceptual vagueness reappears. Finally – and here Blumer expands upon his earlier statement – operationally produced concepts face the serious problem of external validity. Unless their relevance to the empirical world can be established, they are of no use for theory, whose interest lies nowhere else than in that world.

Whether or not these difficulties can be resolved is a question that, rather surprisingly, Blumer leaves open (1954a: 7). At any rate, he proceeds to raise a more fundamental issue, namely, whether nonambiguous, or definitive, concepts are possible in social science. A definitive concept, as Blumer defines it, "refers precisely to what is common to a class of objects, by the aid of a clear definition in terms of attributes or fixed bench marks" (1954a: 7). On the basis of this definition, individual instances of the class can be clearly identified.

By contrast, an ambiguous term, or what Blumer now calls a *sensitizing concept* (1954a: 7), does not enable a clear identification of a specific instance of a class because the definition of the latter lacks fixed experiential attributes. Whereas definitive concepts provide prescriptions of what to see, sensitizing concepts, lacking precise reference, merely suggest general directions along which to look (1954a: 7). The concepts of social science, Blumer asserts, are of a sensitizing rather than a definitive sort.

Having drawn the distinction between the two kinds of concepts, Blumer goes on to consider why the concepts of social science are necessarily of a sensitizing character. The reason centers upon a clash between the formal properties of concepts and of experience: Whereas concepts are universals, experience presents to us only this or that particular object. Already in his 1931 paper, Blumer had commented that our perceptual world is one of particulars (1931: 520). Now he has returned to this feature of experience to work out its implications for a semantic analysis of scientific concepts.

Given his program for a reductive semantics, the universality of concepts and the particularity of experience cannot but exist in a peculiar semantic tension, which Blumer conveys in his notion of the sensitizing concept:

If our empirical world presents itself in the form of distinctive and unique happenings or situations and if we seek through the direct study of this world to establish classes of objects, we are, I think, forced to work with sensitizing concepts (1954a: 8).

Notice in this passage the implied background of theory testing as reductive semantics: Blumer does not say that, given the generality of concepts and the particularity of experience, our *knowledge* of which concepts fit the world depends on a piecemeal testing; rather, he holds that the very *meaning* of those concepts is piecemeal, and therefore ambiguous (i.e., sensitizing).

We must pause to consider whether Blumer's notion of the sensitizing concept is anything more than a cover which masks irreconcilable tendencies. For, it should be asked, how can the universality of concepts be founded upon a semantic procedure which identifies the meaning of a term with the particularism of its reference? Such as a procedure simply dissolves the universal; the latter does not remain even as a sensitizing function.

The conflict between universal and particular simply cannot be resolved within the framework Blumer has employed. And yet he is able to give up neither universal nor particular. To give up the universal character of concepts would be to abrogate intelligibility itself; this was precisely the complaint Blumer had lodged against the form of particularism found in operational definitions. On the other hand, to give up particularism would require transcending his program for reductive semantics, and Blumer is unwilling to do this.

In sum, Blumer is left with something of a dilemma. Yet he manages to evade this dilemma by retreating from the full implications of his analysis. Recall that, in Blumer's view, the most fundamental source of the various deficiencies of social theory is conceptual vagueness. Now, however, he has analyzed vagueness and found it to be rooted in generic features of social scientific concepts. The conclusion would seem to follow that social theory is incorrigibly flawed, but Blumer recoils from such a bleak prognosis.

Instead, he offers hope for a "progressive refinement of sensitizing concepts through careful and imaginative study of the stubborn world to which such concepts are addressed" (1954a: 8). Blumer seems to be saying that conceptual ambiguity is a matter of degree; though social scientific concepts are inevitably sensitizing rather than definitive, they can approach more closely the characteristics of definitive concepts. This is accomplished by naturalistic research, the "direct study" of the social world wherein faithful reportorial depiction of distinctive concrete instances is combined with an analytical probing of their character (1954a: 10).

But notice what has occurred. Initially, Blumer diagnosed the problem of social theory – that is, the breakdown in the interplay of theory, inquiry, and empirical fact – as deriving from ambiguous concepts. Now he is deriving conceptual ambiguity from the breakdown of that interplay. What has happened is that Blumer has unwittingly shifted the locus of the problem. Ironically, his directive for clarifying vague concepts is little more than a restatement of the recommendations he had earlier set aside as not fully adequate. To be sure, Blumer's directive is somewhat more specific than the recommendations he criticized, but it is not different from them in kind.

Blumer has evaded the difficulties inherent in his analysis of conceptual ambiguity by shifting the problem of social theory from vague concepts to bad scientific practice. Because originally the consideration of vague concepts was intended as a theoretical analysis of bad scientific practice, the shift in the focus of concern constitutes an abandonment of the effort to give a theoretical account of that practice. Blumer simply invokes his model of theory testing instead of trying to articulate it.

We should note before leaving the 1954 paper that the notion of the sensitizing concept is, in the context of Blumer's methodological thought, rather anomalous. It departs in important respects from both his earlier and his later thinking. Let us briefly see how.

In the 1931 paper, Blumer had identified as an abuse of scientific concepts their being treated in a "loose, common sense" way, by which he meant that their content was left unspecified and thus sensed rather than comprehended (1931: 532). With the introduction of sensitizing concepts, Blumer modified his earlier view, admitting these concepts to be "grounded on sense instead of on objective traits" (1954a: 9). True, they can still be formulated and communicated, according to Blumer, but not, we might add, in the manner insisted upon in his earlier thought.

In 1955, one year after his introduction of the notion of sensitizing concepts, Blumer read before a professional body (and published) a paper entitled "Attitudes and the social act." In this paper, he identifies as one requirement of a "satisfactory concept in social science" the following: ". . . it must point clearly to the individual instances of the class of empirical objects to which it refers" (1955a: 59). Now, it is just this requirement that a sensitizing concept by definition cannot meet. Blumer's thinking seems to have changed; instead of regarding the concepts of social science as inevitably sensitizing, and the latter as methodologically acceptable, Blumer's view appears to involve the rejection of both opinions.

Additional support for this interpretation is found in a paper published in 1956. There Blumer explicitly mentions the sensitizing concept, but in a critical context. Discussing the shortcomings of variable analysis, Blumer identifies the sensitizing concept as an instance of a pseudo-generic concept (1956: 684). Given that "generic variables are essential . . . to an empirical science" (1956: 684), it follows that sensitizing concepts are not only dispensable, but desirably so.

In sum, the notion of the sensitizing concept appeared somewhat anomalously in the course of Blumer's thinking and disappeared rather quickly. After the 1956 paper, it is not found in his methodological writings. Though it reappears in a response by Blumer to a critic (1977: 286), the mention is brief and rather noncommittal. Whether Blumer came to recognize the serious difficulties involved with the notion is unclear; at any rate, it fades away.

To conclude this section, let us attempt to summarize some of the key moves in Blumer's epistemological endeavors.

In 1939, Blumer's thinking on the validation of scientific theory was tentative and hesitant. Reflecting upon the tension between science and interpretation, he suggested – implicitly, at least – a look-and-see empiricism, founded upon a syntactical and semantic reductionism, but also a number of other validational criteria. Blumer's proposals had an ad hoc quality; there was no trace of systematicity in them. Indeed, he even offered some misgivings in regard to reductive semantics. Moreover, there was a tendency in his thinking, evidenced by his appeal to the expert, to shift the discussion from the criteria of validation to the simple fact of it.

By 1940, Blumer had moved away from his earlier conception of the unity of science. He shifted his reductive semantics to the center of emphasis, attempting to articulate it theoretically by reflecting on the nature of observation in social psychology. Unwittingly, he encountered problems which could not be addressed, much less resolved, within the framework of his empiricism, but he clung to it nonetheless. His perseverance in a refuted framework can be explained, at least in part, by the shift in his discussion from the criteria to the fact of validation.

In 1954, Blumer considered his reductive semantics from another angle, that of the tension between the universality of concepts and the particularity of their empirical referents. The sensitizing concept is the result of his analysis, a result which, as we have seen, is unsatisfactory. Once again, Blumer evaded this conclusion by substituting the fact for the criteria of validation. This substitution, as we will now see, completely dominates, and even defines, the last phase of Blumer's methodological development.

Third phase: Abandoning epistemology

In 1969, Blumer published "The methodological position of symbolic interactionism," a paper frequently regarded as his definitive methodological statement. Blumer himself seems to encourage this view (1969a: viii). Yet, as was indicated in the preface, we need to approach the matter critically. In this section, we will examine chiefly the 1969 paper with an intention to see just how it constitutes an abandonment of methodology as the self-reflection of scientific inquiry.

The frame of inquiry. The section of the paper entitled "Methodological principles of empirical science" (1969b: 21 ff.) begins on an ontological key. Blumer acknowledges that the world can appear to us only in the forms of human images and conceptions, but he denies emphatically that these items are simply equivalent to the world. Rather, the world stands over against our conceptualizations of it, resisting and "talking back" to them.[2] It is this fact that calls for and justifies scientific inquiry. Such inquiry Blumer describes as a "collective quest for answers to questions directed to the resistent character of the given empirical world under study" (1969b: 23). Involved in this quest are a number of different aspects (1969b: 24–6).

First, there is the "possession and use of a prior picture or scheme of the empirical world under study." This picture or scheme orients the entire scientific act, setting the selection and formulation of problems, determining what the data are and how they are to be gathered, specifying the kinds of relations sought between data as well as the forms of propositional statements.

Second, there is an asking of questions of the empirical world and a conversion of these questions into manageable research problems. Here lies the real beginning of the act of inquiry.

Third, there is the determination of what counts as data and the appropriate means for gathering such. These matters are set by the problem. Blumer warns that we vitiate genuine empirical inquiry whenever we allow methods to determine the nature of the data, rather than vice versa.

Fourth, there is the determination of the relations between data. This step yields the findings of the study, so it is especially important to be clear about how relations are established, regardless of the particular methodical procedure employed.

Fifth, there is the interpretation of findings. This terminal step involves relating the results of the study to an outside body of theory. The danger here is that untested or false theories may coerce the interpretation; methodology must attend to ways for avoiding this.

Sixth, there is the use of concepts. Such usage is obviously not a distinct step, but is rather a crucial feature of all previous steps. Thus, concludes Blumer, concepts need especially to be given careful methodological scrutiny. Here we find Blumer returning to his syntactical reductionism to focus upon his favorite unit of analysis.

Treatment of the frame. Blumer's express delineation of the facets of scientific inquiry – or, more accurately, what he perceives to be the "more important" facets – is new with the 1969 paper. What is not new is his methodological treatment of them. According to Blumer's definition, methodology covers the principles that underlie the scientific act. Having specified the facets of this act, Blumer must now grasp them methodologically. And he does so by returning to his look-and-see empiricism.

Yet Blumer's return to this empiricism is marked by a change over the thinking in the previous phase of his development. In that phase, he had made some attempt to articulate his empiricism theoretically, which involved an investigation into some of the features of reductive semantics. As we have seen, Blumer's efforts came to nought; they floundered in evasion and incoherence. In the 1969 paper, Blumer by and large abandons epistemological reflection in favor of procedural inquiry: He describes his empiricism according to how it is done rather than how it is comprehended through underlying principles. This shift virtually abrogates methodological discussion, yet it merely brings to fruition the tendency in Blumer's writings to substitute the fact for the criteria of verification.

We can catch sight of the shift in Blumer's thinking by attending to the following claim:

> The premises of symbolic interactionism are simple. I think they can be readily tested and validated merely by observing what goes on in social life under one's nose (1969b: 50).

The second sentence exemplifies perfectly the spirit of Blumer's look-and-see empiricism. But compare the sentence with Blumer's position in the 1940 paper, where he had probed the complexities of observation and concluded that nonempirical criteria for validating social theory were likely to be necessary (1940: 719). Not only have these criteria disappeared from sight, but Blumer writes as though observation were semantically unproblematic, a very different view from the one presented in the 1940 paper, even though in that paper Blumer had evaded the consequences of his analysis. By 1969, the evasion is all that remains: Having abandoned the attempt to grasp his empiricism theoretically, Blumer simply deploys it.

If Blumer came to shortchange the depth component of methodology, he assuredly does not do the same for the breadth component. That is, he adheres faithfully to the requirement that methodology should embrace the scientific act in its full scope. In specific terms, each of the components of the scientific act that Blumer has identified is to be brought into compliance with his look-and-see empiricism, what he refers to as a "direct examination" of the empirical social world (1969b: 32). This requires each component of the scientific act to be tested according to a two-stage procedure which he labels *exploration* and *inspection* (1969b: 44ff.).

Exploration is a flexible procedure, without fixed protocol, which permits the researcher to gain a close acquaintance with a sphere of social life while simultaneously grounding each component of the scientific act securely in that life. The focus of study is initially quite broad, but it narrows as knowledge is acquired. The researcher approaches an area, examines it, develops new perspectives and lines of inquiry, and, on the basis of enriched understanding, decides what data are relevant to the research problem (1969b: 40).

In terms of specific techniques, exploration employs anything that appears to be helpful, including direct observation, interviewing persons, listening to their conversations, using life-histories, letters, diaries, public records, counts of relevant items, and staging group discussions (1969b: 41). The only constraint on procedures and techniques is that imposed by standards of ethics.

Though exploration has no set protocol, Blumer makes several suggestions that serve as guiding principles. First, the researcher is well advised to seek out participants in a sphere of life who are knowledgeable about that sphere; such persons are likely to be more useful to the researcher than are participants selected through representative sampling. Informed participants, gathered together to discuss their sphere of life, offer an especially valuable resource for exploratory research.

Another guiding principle derives from the need for the researcher to test and constantly revise, as necessary, his or her understanding of the area under study. Part of this process occurs through observation of and interaction with participants. Yet, since the researcher is interested in aspects of social life not known to informants, some other means is necessary in order to achieve research goals. Blumer borrows from Charles Darwin two suggestions for aiding the researcher in his or her effort not to remain captive to preconceptions. First, it is useful to entertain questions even of a seemingly ludicrous character. Through such self-questioning new perspectives can become visible. The second suggestion is to record both the observations that challenge one's conceptions as well as those which seem odd or otherwise interesting though unrelated to one's conceptions. Recorded observations of both sorts can be of great help in the subsequent redirecting of thought.

Exploratory research aims for an accurate and comprehensive account of a sphere of social life. Frequently, according to Blumer, such an account will provide answers to theoretical questions, or it may occasionally obviate the need for invoking any theory to explain what originally was problematic. Yet exploration is not the terminal stage of research; a further effort, which Blumer calls inspection, is required.

Empirical science does not rest satisfied with descriptive familiarity, but seeks theoretical propositions composed of clear, discriminating concepts set in specified relations. Importantly, the analytic component must be grounded empirically, and inspection is the procedure Blumer proposes to accomplish this.

Inspection involves an "intensive focused examination of the empirical content" of concepts and their relations (1969b: 43). The prototype of this procedure is the handling of a physical object that is not yet known; we may pick up the object, turn it over, look at it closely from different angles, raise questions about it, and reexamine it in light of these questions (1969b: 44). Inspection is a close and shifting scrutiny that, like exploration, has no set protocol; both procedures call for flexibility and imagination on the part of the researcher.

Through inspection the nature of analytical elements is established (1969b: 44); the process is one of disengaging and refining universals through close scrutiny of their empirical instances. Blumer still views this procedure through the lens of his reductive semantics. Empirical meaning, he tells us, exists

. . . in a specification that allows one to go to the empirical world and say securely in the case of any empirical thing that this is an instance of a concept and that is not (1969b: 45).

Such meaning constitutes one of the requirements Blumer specifies for scientific analysis (1969b: 43), namely, the need for "clear, discriminating analytical elements." And these elements are generally lacking in social science (1969b: 45).

Blumer returns once more to his familiar complaint about the vague and ambiguous character of social scientific concepts. Only now he identifies as the source of the problem the "failure to employ the procedure of inspection'' (1969b: 45). In one sense, this identification merely refines what Blumer had recommended in both the 1940 and 1954 papers. Yet it also departs from the portions of those papers which attempted to grasp the problem theoretically. The sensitizing concept, for instance, pointed to the semantic tension between universal and particular; that concept is nowhere to be found in the 1969 paper. Instead, Blumer writes as though procedural matters alone could solve all conceptual problems rather than, as earlier, that generic features of concepts accounted for those ''problems.'' The 1969 paper represents the final victory of method over methodology in Blumer's general program.

Against methodical apriorism. Through exploration and inspection, then, each component of the scientific act is to be empirically tested. Moreover, such testing of each component is to be performed *independently* of the testing of the other components (1969b: 32). Since Blumer's thinking on this requirement is pivotal for his empiricism, we need to consider it carefully, although first some preliminary considerations are necessary.

Science for Blumer, as we have seen, is a collective quest to extract answers to questions directed toward the world's obdurate facticity. Thus, it is that facticity which has the final word for scientific inquiry. This final word encompasses each and every component of the scientific act; none is exempt from the judgment of empirical testing. ''Reality,'' as Blumer insists, ''exists in the empirical world and not in the methods used to study that world'' (1969b: 27). Consequently, the only value of methods or techniques lies in their instrumentality for investigating the world (1969b: 27).

Blumer's position, in a word, is one of unbridled opposition to methodical apriorism, the view that scientific inquiry entails certain fixed and set procedures or methods. Furthermore, he finds social science rife with this fault. One of its forms consists in the injunction to cast the social world ''in terms of the findings of advanced physical science'' (1969b: 23). Blumer counters that this injunction is ''philosophical doctrinizing'' which forces the world to fit a given scheme; as such it is not in the spirit of ''genuine empirical science'' (1969b: 23). We see clearly that, in contrast to his earlier thinking, Blumer is now totally disinclined toward accepting the procedural unity of the sciences.

Pressing forward his attack on methodical apriorism, Blumer includes within that designation some of the most widely deployed schemes of research in social science. He specifically identifies and responds critically to four approaches that purport to constitute proper empirical testing.

First, there is the adherence to research protocol. By the latter Blumer means simply the standardized principles of research design. It is his view that these principles can embrace distorted components of the scientific act, such as "false premises, erroneous problems, distorted data, spurious relations, inaccurate concepts, and unverified interpretations" (1969b: 29). What is worse, Blumer contends, is that research protocol contains no self-correcting mechanism to detect when these components have gone empirically astray. The established principles of research design thus coerce rather than respect the empirical world, Blumer concludes.

Second, there is the replication of research studies. The problem here is that, if a given protocol is not self-correcting, the repeated use of it will not be either.

Third, there is the reliance on testing hypotheses, the principle scheme of current research in the social and psychological sciences (1969b: 29). Hypothesis testing, in its logical essentials, approaches the world as if it had a certain makeup and then checks to see if the predicted consequences of such makeup are actually found. Blumer allows that there is a "measure of truth" to the model of hypothesis testing, but only if the hypothesis genuinely epitomizes the theory from which it is deduced and if a scrupulous search is made for evidence that could disconfirm the hypothesis. These two conditions, Blumer argues, are infrequently met, with the result that theoretical schemes have exhibited a notorious ease with which they are "verified" – and occasionally even an ability to survive when some hypotheses derived from them are not confirmed. On the basis of its past record, Blumer recommends wariness concerning the adequacy of hypothesis testing for empirical validation of the components of the scientific act.

The fourth and final research procedure consists in the use of operational definitions. Here Blumer returns to an old target of his criticism, though this time his remarks are somewhat truncated. He points out that, if a theoretical concept is held to refer to something that is present in the empirical world, research attention must be devoted to the various forms of such presence in order to be adequate to the concept. Operational procedures arbitrarily limit the empirical reference of a concept and thus, in their own way, distort the empirical world.

All four research schemes, to summarize Blumer's argument, either constitute or facilitate something inimical to the proper course of empirical science: They act as "governing agents . . . forcing research to serve their character and bending the empirical world to their premises" (1969b: 33). In consequence, social research is an arena for the "grand display and clash of social philosophies" (1969b: 33).

Blumer views methodical apriorism not solely and simply as an intellectual fault of social scientists, whether individually or collectively, but, perhaps more ominously, as a tendency rooted in the social context of social research. In particular, Blumer identifies the determination of such research by government agencies as especially conducive to the curtailment of the full empirical responsiveness required of science (1967a: 158ff.) Typically, according to Blumer, agency-determined research

excludes several vital parts of the research enterprise from scrutiny, challenge, and correction by the participating scientists. I refer to the selection of the problem that the project is to study, the premises that underlie the formulation of the problem, and the dominant ideas that give the study its character and its direction. These are obviously matters that are determined by the agency in response to its practical interests and ends – and they are not devised to satisfy the interests of science (1967a: 159).

Such interests, for Blumer, stem from the one central maxim of scientific praxis: "the free pursuit of truth, wherever it may lead" (1967a: 158). To the extent to which the social scientist

has closed to him the right to scrutinize critically and challenge any or all of these parts of the scientific undertaking, he is forced to forfeit in corresponding measure the pursuit of truth. Within those areas of the scientific undertaking that are closed to his critical assessment he becomes a technician – an executor carrying out a predesigned task in place of being a seeker of knowledge (1967a: 158).

Blumer sees agency-determined research as contributing to the corruption of social science qua science – that is, to the undermining of the central maxim of science – largely through the very tangible enticements with which it lures social scientists into complicity with one form or other of methodical apriorism (1967a: 167ff.). To counter this pernicious influence is a responsibility Blumer places upon professional organizations of social scientists (1967a: 173). What is significant about this entire discussion is that to which it attests, if only in the manner of adumbration: Methodology as the self-reflection of scientific inquiry with a normative intent readily passes over into a criticism of the social organization of science. Blumer, having touched upon this matter, unfortunately does nothing further with it.

Blumer's opposition to methodical apriorism reveals just how far he had come from the early phase of his reflection. As his thought grew more and more dominated by his empiricism, he abandoned the notion of any inherent unity of the sciences (cf. 1969b: 23) as an instance of methodical apriorism. Such apriorism was viewed as encompassing what in his dissertation Blumer had referred to as the functional aspect of science. Instead of holding that aspect in normative superordination over scientific inquiry per se, he now viewed it as a method, not as methodology. And methods, in view of Blumer's empiricism, are not prescribed *a priori* but must be chosen and evaluated solely in accordance with their suitability for studying a given segment of the empirical world. Consequently, it is not permissible to dismiss peremptorily the research procedures of symbolic interactionism as somehow "unscientific"; it is the world, not speculative fiat, which is to decide the matter.

Apriorism and holism. Blumer's opposition to methodical apriorism took him even beyond the denial that science inherently requires this or that specific technique or procedure; he was in fact led to a methodological assault upon the notion of methodical holism. The result of this assault is the disconnection of the scientific act, a consequence receiving expression in Blumer's requirement that the different facets of inquiry be tested *independently* (1969b: 28, 32). Although Blumer does not explicitly state the rationale which underpins his disconnection of the scientific act, we can reconstruct it quite readily as an outgrowth of his look-and-see empiricism.

That empiricism, to recall, was conceived as a reductive semantics, disallowing any semantic input "from above," that is, from abstract conceptualizations removed from the immediacy of direct experience. Such input signaled to Blumer an apriorism antithetical to the nature of empiricism. It is indeed this same semantic reductionism which prompts him to disconnect the scientific act: Abstract principles of method or of underlying theoretical schemes are held to coerce the empirical world, twisting and forcing it to fit their semantic prescriptions rather than respecting its nature. In order to achieve such respect, each substantive portion of the scientific act, separately considered, needs to be semantically founded on direct experience. We might term this requirement *methodical atomism*.

Blumer failed, as we have seen, to articulate his empiricism theoretically. This might lead us to expect a similar fate for methodical atomism, which is after all only a specification of that empiricism in the context of the scientific act. And, true enough, Blumer does indeed encounter a serious problem with his methodical atomism: He finds it in practice unworkable, and quickly resorts to methodical holism.

That holism, in fact, receives explicit sanction by Blumer. "The entire act of scientific study," he says, "is oriented and shaped by the underlying picture of the empirical world that is used" (1969b: 25). Such a picture steers the formulation of problems, the characterization and gathering of data, the sorts of relations sought between the data, and the formal construction of propositions (1969b: 25). In short, the entire scientific act feels the "fundamental and pervasive effect wielded . . . by the initiating picture of the empirical world" (1969b: 25).

Blumer goes on to articulate this holism for the specific case of symbolic interactionism (1969b: 50ff.) in a more thoroughgoing manner than was the case in his 1937 effort. He identifies four central tenets of the interactionist perspective and elucidates their implications for research.

First, symbolic interactionism holds that people, individually and collectively, act according to the meanings that are given to the objects composing their worlds (1969b: 50). This implies that research, in order to understand action, must get at those meanings, that is, must view the world from the standpoint of the participants involved in the action. To achieve this understanding requires several things, the first of which is the ability to take the roles of others, a skill requiring cultivation. Second, "subjective" understanding requires a body of relevant observations. These are not produced by standard research devices such as "questionnaires, polls, scales, use of survey research items, or the setting of predesignated variables" (1969b: 51); instead, relevant observations consist of descriptive accounts by actors of how they refer to objects. To guard against distortions in the accounts of particular individuals, Blumer includes as a "must" a "critical collective discussion by a group of well-informed participants in the given world" under study (1969b: 52). Third, "subjective" understanding requires researchers to be constantly on guard against projecting their own understanding of objects upon other people.

The second tenet of symbolic interactionism holds that social life is a process wherein actors make indications to one another and interpret the indications made by others. Interaction, whether between individuals or collectives, is built up sequentially in a reciprocal display of gesture and interpretation. Thus, interaction is a social emergent as well as a formative force in its own right.

For research, all of this implies, first, a rejection of any methodical approach that treats social interaction as "merely the medium through which determining factors produce behavior" (1969b: 53). Sociologists tend frequently to regard behavior as a function of such things as role, status, norm, value, etc.; psychologists, on the other hand, impute causal efficacy to such items as drives, need-dispositions, attitudes, unconscious motives, etc. Yet in both cases the underlying scheme of research is the same; social interaction is methodically emasculated, Blumer contends.

Additionally, the second tenet of symbolic interactionism suggests a lack of warrant for viewing social interaction in terms of any one fixed form, such as cooperation, conflict, or whatever. Interaction is fluid and variable; in any event, its form is to be discovered empirically, not pre-scribed in advance.

The third tenet of symbolic interactionism – closely related to the first two – holds that social action, both individual and collective, involves a constructing process "in which the actors note, interpret, and assess the situations confronting them" (1969b: 50). Since social action is for Blumer the "primary subject matter of social science" (1969b: 55), the categories of action are methodically decisive. For research they imply that attention should be focused upon the process in which action is con-structed, taking the role of the actor, noting what he or she takes into account, how it is interpreted, and how, through selection, alternatives are eliminated to lead finally to action (1969b: 56).

The fourth tenet of symbolic interactionism involves its view of the molar forms of social organization – such things as institutions, stratifica-tion arrangements, divisions of labor, corporate units, and so on. The interactionist perspective views these forms as "arrangements of people who are interlinked in their respective actions" (1969b:58). The organiza-tion of a given molar unit, in short, is constituted by the concatenation of numerous persons' social actions taking place at different points (1969b: 58). This view differs sharply with those sociological approaches which treat molar units as entities operating according to their own systemic dynamics, the latter expressing themselves through their human partici-pants. The interactionist view refuses to reduce social activity to the sta-tus of an inert dependent variable; instead, "it seeks explanation in the way in which participants define, interpret, and meet the situations at their respective points" (1969b: 58).

Methodically, then, the study of social organizations requires no dis-tinct form of research for the interactionist. Blumer does make two com-ments specifically pertinent to organization research. First, that research needs to look beneath organizational norms and rules to the "two concur-rent processes in which people are defining each other's perspectives and the individual, through self-interaction, is redefining his own perspec-tive" (1969b: 59). Second, since joint action is generally linked temporally with previous joint action, organization research needs to be directed to historical, as well as contemporaneous, linkages.

Such are the general directives for social research that Blumer derives from the symbolic interactionist perspective. It is in these directives that his methodical holism receives expression. Yet, as we have already noted, methodologically Blumer espouses an atomism wherein the various aspects of the scientific act are tested independently (1969b: 32). In brief, Blumer's method and his methodology are at odds.

The logical status of symbolic interactionism. One final problem with the 1969 paper requires attention. The source of that problem is the juxtaposition of methodological discussion with the tenets of symbolic interactionism. Blumer treats the latter in its logical properties as merely one theoretical perspective among others (1969b: 21); that is, he holds the methodological principles of empirical science to be logically distinct from the precepts of symbolic interactionism. Methodology is the court of appeal for interactionism as well as all other scientific theories.

The problem with this view is that interactionism in several of its tenets is logically on the same level of reflection with methodology. For example, interactionism offers a semantic theory in which meaning is depicted as a social construction (1969b: 4ff.). In that context Blumer repudiates the view of "realist" semantics in which meaning, inherent in the thing that has it, "needs merely to be disengaged by observing the objective thing that has the meaning" (1969b: 4). Yet such a view is precisely the tendency operating in Blumer's methodological statements where they seek to found empiricism on a reductive semantics. Since reductive semantics and interactionist semantics are both theories of meaning per se, they are on the same logical level. Located there, they are simply inconsistent.

Blumer's disconnection of methodology and symbolic interactionism can be seen in the very organization of the 1969 paper. The latter comprises three sections: "The nature of symbolic interactionism," "Methodological principles of empirical science," and "Methodological orientation." In the first section, Blumer surveys the interactionist perspective; in the second, he discusses some ontological and – implicitly at least – epistemological principles underlying scientific inquiry; in the third, Blumer works out the implications of interactionism for research (i.e., its methodical holism). This neat compartmentalization crumbles once we recognize that interactionism crosses over into methodology.

The tendency to disconnect methodological reflection proper and symbolic interactionism is deeply rooted in Blumer's thinking; it pervades the phase of his semantic inquiries in that none of the methodological tenets of that period are especially indebted to interactionism. Only in his first paper, "Science without concepts," did Blumer advance a methodological scheme drawing from the interactionist perspective; yet, as we have seen, at that early stage Blumer had not hit upon his characteristic empiricism. The advent of the latter occurred outside the interactionist frame. In one important sense, Blumer's third phase, as exemplified in "The methodological position of symbolic interactionism," represents a synthesis of the first two phases: his empiricism for the first time appears jointly with his interactionism. We have noted how badly the union fares.

Notes

1 Note that this last point is actually inconsistent with the thrust of Blumer's argument. To assert that time-held concepts, though vague, are likely to denote something significant, is to gainsay the earlier contention that vagueness undermines the very source of significance in science: the working relationship between theory and research.

2 For a discussion of Blumer's ontology, see Chapter 3, "Ontological Repair."

3. Critical extensions

In Chapter 2 we followed the development of Blumer's methodology, critically noting a number of problems. In this chapter I want to press the criticism a little further by relating selected themes in Blumer's thought to a broader philosophical discussion. At issue here is the *overall* meaning and tenability of Blumer's methodological project.

Beyond look-and-see empiricism

We shall begin the critical extensions by addressing sequentially three questions, for Blumer's mistaken answers (implicit or explicit) to these questions bear heavy responsibility for misleading him.

1. Does the vocabulary of a workable scientific language admit to full semantic reduction to experiential givens?
2. If not, what is the role of that language which is semantically nonreducible?
3. What is the epistemological status of the nonreducible language?

Swan song for reductive semantics. The first question, whether the vocabulary of a workable scientific language can be semantically reduced to the givens of experience, is fruitfully addressed by considering the development of logical positivism. This positivism sprang boldly upon the scene with a simple prescription for curing the ills of philosophy. According to Rudolph Carnap, the advances in "applied logic," whose aim is to clarify the cognitive content of scientific statements by means of logical analysis, had led to a positive and a negative result. On the positive side, the concepts of science are clarified in that their "formal–logical and epistemological connections are made explicit." Conversely:

In the domain of *metaphysics,* including all philosophy of value and normative theory, logical analysis yields the negative result *that the alleged statements in this domain are entirely meaningless* (Carnap 1932: 60–61).

Both results, positive and negative, stem from a logical analysis which clarifies the conditions of possibility for any cognitively meaningful language. Since language consists of a vocabulary and a syntax, cognitive significance may be lost in either or both of two ways: A sentence may employ one or more meaningless words, or it may connect them in a counter-syntactical way. Let us look closely at the first of these cases.

The meaning of a word, Carnap argues, depends upon two conditions (1932: 62). First, the syntax of the word must be fixed (i.e., how it occurs in its simplest sentence form, its elementary sentence, must be specified). The elementary sentence for the word "pen," for example, is "x is a pen." Second, the elementary sentence (S) containing the word must permit an answer to the following question, which can be formulated *equivalently* in four ways:

(1.) What sentences is S *deducible* from, and what sentences are deducible from S?
(2.) Under what conditions is S supposed to be true, and under what conditions false?
(3.) How is S to be verified?
(4.) What is the *meaning* of S? (Carnap 1932: 62).

More directly,

. . . every word of the language is reduced to other words and finally to the words which occur in the so-called 'observation sentences' or 'protocol sentences.' It is through this reduction that the word acquires its meaning (Carnap 1932: 63).

Applying this criterion to the vocabulary of traditional areas of philosophy, the positivists rejected as cognitively meaningless such disciplines as metaphysics, ethics, and aesthetics. This, as Carnap indicated, was the negative result of logical analysis. But, on its positive side, the analysis was supposed to contribute to the domain of empirical science through a clarification of its concepts. We need to consider just how this program fared.

Initially, the positivist account of scientific theory treated theoretical terms as fully definable on the basis of observation terms (Suppe 1977: 12). Yet it soon became apparent that this requirement was too restrictive; it dissolved the universality of terms in a particularism of operations (just as Blumer had seen in his critique of operational definitions), and disposition terms could not be accommodated (Suppe 1977: 20).[1] To handle these problems, the reductive criterion for cognitive meaning – the significance criterion – was relaxed. Carnap proposed that theory terms be permitted which are experientially defined only in part (Suppe 1977:

21; cf. Hempel 1950: 120). Yet the relaxed criterion still proved too restrictive, for it disallowed terms of certain "advanced scientific theories" – terms such as "absolute temperature," "gravitational potential," "electric field," etc. – which could be introduced neither through experiential definitions nor reduction sentences (Hempel 1950: 121). These terms required a weakening of the significance criterion as applied to scientific theories.

In its final version, positivism construed scientific theories – at least those of the "advanced type" – as "hypothetico-deductive systems in which all statements are logical consequences of a set of fundamental assumptions" (Hempel 1950: 121). These systems in their logical structure are equivalent to the axiomatized uninterpreted systems of mathematics and logic. What renders them theories of empirical science is an empirical interpretation given to *some* of their sentences, often derived rather than fundamental ones. Thus, it is the system as a whole which acquires empirical significance through experiential interpretations of some of its parts. These parts indirectly interpret the others empirically.

In regard to the meaning of a cognitively significant sentence, Hempel tells us that:

. . . the cognitive meaning of a statement in empiricist language is reflected in the totality of its logical relationships to all other statements in that language and not to observation sentences alone. In this sense, the statements of empirical science have a surplus meaning over and above what can be expressed in terms of relevant observation sentences (1950: 123).

Given the recognition of such "surplus meaning," it is little wonder that Hempel was soon to suggest that the idea of cognitive significance, with its sharp bifurcation of significant and nonsignificant sentences, had lost its usefulness and needed to be replaced with normative criteria which admit of differences not in *kind*, but in *degree* (1950: 129).

The development of logical positivism effectively attests to the failure of its original program. The language of science proved irreducible to a lexicon of observables; instead, it was found to require recourse to a nonempirical metalanguage (Suppe 1977: 35), the locus of Hempel's "surplus meaning." The lesson to be drawn for epistemology is that empiricism cannot be founded in the manner that the early positivists had desired.

In the Blumer secondary literature, the parallels between the vicissitudes of logical positivism and Blumer's own epistemological ventures have gone unrecognized. Both Blumer and the early positivists sought to equate verification and meaning, which is to construe epistemology on the foundation of reductive semantics. Both Blumer and the positivists, in turn, faced the dilemmas of executing this program. Though early on Blumer had certain misgivings about the adequacy of a reductive semantics (cf. 1939: 162), these misgivings did not forestall him from embarking upon his doomed empiricism.

We have surveyed the results. Blumer's tendency in both the 1940 and 1954 papers was to pursue reflection upon his empiricism to the point where serious problems for it arose, and then to evade those problems by shifting the discussion strictly to a methodical level. Finally, in his third phase, he abandoned epistemology and fell flatly into the clutches of his empiricism, construed *methodically.* By contrast, the positivists handled the dilemmas of their original program by adjusting it piecemeal until, eventually, the original was no more. In short, they corrected their errors, or at least some of them, while Blumer remained in thrall to his own. In criticism of Blumer, we can draw profitably upon the positivists' self-transcendence and jettison reductive semantics.

The super-sensible element in knowledge.   The idea that science, or indeed knowledge in general, involves reliance on nonempirical semantic resources is hardly original with late positivism. On the contrary, it is an insight indigenous to epistemological rationalism, almost as old as philosophy itself. We can pick up this line of thought in Plato. In the dialogue *Theaetetus,* the discussion turns to consider the thesis that "knowledge is perception." Rebutting such a view, Plato's Socrates offers the following argument.

Each of the senses gives us its own characteristic "object," and it is not conceivable that one sense can give us the distinctive "object" of another sense. The bitterness given by taste, for example, cannot be gotten through sight or hearing or touch. Each sensory faculty has its own distinctive predicates corresponding to its own disparate "objects." Where a common predicate is applied to these objects, therefore, it cannot be derived from any particular sense but must belong to a common "sense," which is the mind itself. Native predicates of the mind include such concepts as "existence," "difference," "sameness," "unity," and so on. Thus, concludes the argument, ". . . the mind contemplates some things through its own instrumentality, others through the bodily faculties" (Plato 1961: 890).

Skipping two millennia, we can pick up this argument in another rationalist philosopher, Leibniz. According to him, there are three grades of notions:

. . . the *sensible only*, which are the objects appropriate to each sense in particular; *the sensible and at the same time intelligible*, which pertain to the common sense; and the *intelligible only*, which belong to the understanding (1951: 359).

At the first level of notions, those which are purely sensible, we find the objects of the particular senses: colors, sounds, odors, flavors, and the qualities of touch. These "objects" are indeed given by the senses, but the latter provide no assistance for *understanding* what these sensible qualities are or in what they consist. Familiar but not understood, sensible qualities are in fact occult qualities, and require "notions more manifest to render them explicable" (1951: 356).

For a quality to be understood, we at least need a definition of it. And purely sensible qualities admit of no definitions: The color "blue," for example, cannot be given a definition which provides marks sufficient for recognizing the thing designated. "Blue" serves as its own mark; it must be perceived visually to be "understood." While such seeing may render the notion clear – using Leibniz's terminology – it does not render the notion distinct, for seeing does not provide the sufficient basis for a discursive account of the matter.

Such account requires ascension to the next grade of knowledge, to those notions of the common sense both sensible and intelligible. Leibniz explains the common sense in the following way:

As therefore our soul compares (for example) the numbers and figures which are in colors with the numbers and figures which are found by touch, there must be an *internal sense*, in which the perceptions of these different external senses are found united. This is what is called *imagination*, which comprises at once *the notions of the particular senses*, which are *clear* but *confused*, and the notions of the *common sense*, which are clear and distinct (1951: 357).

What endows the notions of the common sense with their intelligibility is an admixture of the third grade of notions, those purely intelligible concepts of the understanding. The locus in which sensible notions are fused with intelligible notions Leibniz refers to as the imagination. This faculty represents a synthesizing function in which experience is forged from the lower and higher grades of notions. Immanuel Kant was later to develop this insight, in the *Critique of Pure Reason*, in elaborate detail (1965: cf. especially 129ff.).

What the rationalists offer – in considering our second question – is a view as to the function of nonempirical concepts. Put generally, that function is to make experience intelligible. As we have seen, the late phase of logical positivism was also led to admit as much. One important difference between the positivists and the rationalists lies in the manner in which each construed the general function of nonempirical concepts. The rationalists viewed them as entering synthetically into the very tissue of experience, such that anything perceived, and also articulable, is always already concept-laden. The positivists, by contrast, did not go so far, limiting their discussion of the nature of experience to the question of whether the "given" should receive a phenomenalistic or a physicalistic interpretation (Carnap 1932: 63; Suppe 1977: 45). The strict bifurcation of theory and observation remained virtually unchanged throughout the development of positivism (Suppe 1977: 45). This bifurcation, with its implicit notion that an observation term is intersubjectively nonproblematic with regard to its truth, has been scathingly criticized by postpositivist philosophers of science (cf. Suppe 1977: 80ff.), and in consequence widely rejected. Today, the notion that observation is theory-laden has become something of a commonplace. The rationalists, at least to this extent, are vindicated.

Corrigible synthesis.   We may recall that Blumer's first paper, "Science without concepts," provided a view of experience as a synthetic achievement. Nonempirical concepts were held to introduce semantic determinations from "above" in such a manner that the perceptual field was reorganized and new objects were "created" (1931: 527). Since for Blumer this view of experience derives from pragmatist psychology (1931: 518), it suggests a point of articulation between that psychology and methodology proper. But Blumer quickly severed the link, embracing in its place his look-and-see empiricism.

The rationale underlying that shift warrants close scrutiny, since in effect it misled Blumer's subsequent methodological efforts. To gather that rationale we must return to the review of *The Polish Peasant,* for it is in that pivotal document that we encounter Blumer at the crossroads. Semantic determination from "above," his thinking went, is tantamount to the determination of experience *a priori.* It is this fateful equation that drove Blumer from a synthetic account of experience, since at the methodological level he construed the decisive feature of empirical science as its denial of *a priori* determinations. But here we must pause to ask: Did Blumer not overshoot his mark? Is a rejection of apriorism in science necessarily a rejection of experiential synthesis? Critical reflection here leads toward an answer to the third of our initial questions.

Blumer's equation suggests a proximity which lends it intelligibility: In the epistemology of rationalism, experiential synthesis was indeed held to be synthesis *a priori*. Traditionally, the rationalists regarded nonempirical concepts as innate ideas, although with Kant that view was discarded and replaced with the functional requirements of synthesis per se. In either case, however, the designation of synthesis as *a priori* is mistaken, and, against both Blumer and the rationalists, we need to understand why.

The answer lies partially in the way that the notion of the *a priori* has been grasped. That notion, meaning, in its strongest sense, universal and necessary, became somewhat diluted in rationalist usage. Together, universality and necessity comprise two analytically distinguishable aspects: internal incorrigibility and external incorrigibility (Korner 1970: 14ff.). The first relates the incorrigibility of a concept or proposition to a specific categorial framework such that to reject the concept or proposition is to reject the framework. External incorrigibility refers to the incorrigibility of a concept or proposition with respect to *any* categorial framework which might be employed.

The rationalists tended to confine the notion of the *a priori* to the former aspect. Thus the defect of their arguments which purported to be *a priori* in the full-bodied sense

is their failure to provide a uniqueness proof, i.e., the demonstration that the categorial framework is universal. Kant and others seem to have been under the illusion that the exhibition of their own categorial framework already includes the proof of its uniqueness (Korner 1970: 72).

In short, rationalist epistemology articulated certain immanent necessities of thought systems without proving those systems themselves to be necessary. In consequence, the rationalist notion of the *a priori* fell short of its mark.

Given the absence of a uniqueness-proof, we are not constrained to regard any categorial framework (including whatever deductive systems it may employ) as *a priori*. This opens the door for an *empiricist* appropriation of certain traditionally rationalist insights, including especially the super-sensible element of knowledge and its function in the synthesis of experience. Of course, the key to any empiricist appropriation lies in the specification of external corrigibility as involving experiential testing. It was in fact the fear that this is not possible which goaded Blumer toward his look-and-see empiricism. In the following section we shall examine theory testing in order to see that Blumer's fear was unfounded.

Testing theory. The move beyond look-and-see empiricism implies a considerable modification of Blumer's view of theory verification (and verifiability). The tendency in Blumer is to treat experience as univocally manifesting the nature of things, with science, therefore, having only to respect the methodical requirement of unbiased observation in order to glimpse the world's truth. Failure to reach this univocal truth follows from a failure to observe carefully enough, and, since careful observation is the quintessence of empiricism, failure to arrive at the true nature of things is tantamount to the abandonment of empiricism.

We can see all of this in Blumer's paper "Psychological import of the human group" (1953), which begins as follows:

> The aim of this paper is to stress the need of respecting the nature of human group life in formulating social psychological theories and schemes of research. . . . Most conceptions of the human group which are present today in our field are not formed through careful empirical study of human association, but are primarily projections of notions or schemes derived from other sources. . . . Faithful regard for the nature of human association would require, I suspect, the alteration and rejection of many ideas and practices which are stock in trade today among social psychologists (1953: 185).

Blumer goes on to identify and criticize four ways in which social psychologists arrive at their theoretical conceptions of human association; he then presents his own view, the true (i.e., "empirically adequate") notion of such association.

What is methodologically significant here is the way Blumer equates "empirical verification" with "careful observation to disclose the [one true] nature of an object." We find this equation again in the 1969 paper where Blumer cites as evidence of theoretical and methodical apriorism

> . . . the array of conflicting schemes as to the nature and composition of human society and the conspicuous ease with which adherents of each scheme 'validate' the scheme through their own research (1969b: 33).

The implication, again, is that genuinely empirical research obviates the prospect of divergent theoretical orientations, and where these orientations flourish, there is not, consequently, genuine empirical inquiry, but rather some form of apriorism. At bottom this thinking is similar to the positivist notion that science's (non-logical) language comprises only protocol sentences, whose truth is intersubjectively nonproblematic.

Once we move beyond positivist empiricism, the account of theory verification and verifiability requires extensive rethinking. In the first place, the recognition of theoretical terms which are semantically emergent vis-à-vis observation implies that no strict relationship holds wherein "fact" entails theory. This view, that scientific theories are inevitably *underde-*

termined by facts, is rather standard fare in current philosophy of science (Hesse 1978: 1).

Second, the interpretation of experience as a synthetic achievement (i.e., of observation as theory-laden), implies a certain reflexivity to theory testing. Since data are data relative to some theory, the latter is, in a sense, tested in terms of itself. Lest such reflexivity suggest an immanent-ism of vicious circularity – an external incorrigibility – it must be qualified in the following manner. First, theory may call for certain data which experience may or may not be obliging enough to provide. The experiential absence of predicted data would tend to raise doubts about the adequacy of the theory being tested. Second, the theory-ladenness of data does not imply that only the particular theory being tested provides the semantic input for observation. On the contrary, any theory may "impregnate" data. Moreover, alternative theories may produce data relevant to the testing of a competing theory:

Not only is the description of every single fact dependent on some *theory* (which may, of course, be very different from the theory to be tested), but there also exist facts which cannot be unearthed except with the help of alternatives to the theory to be tested, and which become unavailable as soon as such alternatives are excluded. This suggests that the methodological unit to which we must refer when discussing questions of test and empirical content is constituted by a *whole set of partly overlapping, factually adequate, but mutually inconsistent* theories (Feyerabend 1975: 1939).

In this way of thinking, theory avoids a sterile immanentism through its confrontation with data opened up by competing theories. Given the theory-laden character of data, such confrontation is indeed essential to the process of *empirical* testing itself.

All of this – a broadened version of empiricism – suggests a perspective in which our knowledge of the world is viewed in terms of

an ever increasing ocean of mutually incompatible (and perhaps even incommensurable) alternatives, each single theory, each fairy tale, each myth that is part of the collection forcing the others into greater articulation and all of them contributing via this process of competition, to the development of our consciousness (Feyerabend 1975: 30).

Scientific knowledge, then, cannot be treated in the manner common to both early positivism and Blumer, that is, in terms of dichotomous evaluative criteria (significant/nonsignificant or even true/false). Rather, the picture is blurred, and any normative standard will have to admit of degree. Science presents – synchronically, diachronically, or both – an array of different and conflicting theories, most of which have at least some evidential support. In assigning gradations of merit through the testing of theory, it is important not to overlook, as Feyerabend would remind us, how the conflict of theories itself contributes to that assignment.

The sociality of knowledge.   Thus far we have considered several points of critical extension in regard to Blumer's epistemological stance, respecting that stance as empiricist while also recognizing the need for a tenable version of empiricism. Toward that end we added the super-sensible component of knowledge and considered what follows for the problem of testing theory. Now, within the extended frame of reference, we can proceed to address two problems noted in the previous chapter: the inconsistency in Blumer between methodical atomism and methodical holism, and his disconnection of methodology and symbolic interactionism. The former problem, since it can be handled without any modification of the empiricist scheme already proposed, will be taken up in Chapter 4. In what follows we consider the second problem, for it requires a supplementation to our methodological extension.

In Chapter 2, we saw that Blumer tends to disconnect methodological discussion proper from the position of symbolic interactionism, treating the latter as simply one scientific theory among others, albeit an evidentially more defensible one. We noted also why such disconnection is untenable: Interactionism offers a theory of meaning incompatible with the reductive semantics of a look-and-see empiricism. In one aspect, we have already proposed a reconnection of methodology and interactionism by providing for an empiricism that contains a key element common to both: a synthetic view of experience. Yet, in another aspect, our discussion is incomplete, for it has not touched on a crucial area of the interactionist view of language and linguistic understanding: its social character. Thus, to complete the reconnection of methodology and interactionism, we need to delve into the social side of epistemology.

It will be helpful to begin by identifying a pivotal opposition that divides Blumer's reductionist and interactionist models of language and understanding. The guiding question is, how does each model construe the nature of objectivity (intersubjectivity)?

Reductionist semantics locates the meaning of a word in something (sense datum, physical thing) given immediately to the senses. Thus, the locus of objectivity is there in the given itself. On this view, it is quite conceivable to imagine a solitary knowing subject arriving at objective knowledge of the world. This assumption can be viewed as *methodological solipsism* (Apel 1977: 297ff.).

Such solipsism is indeed standard in the epistemological tradition, not only on its empiricist side, but on its rationalist side from Descartes to Husserl as well (Apel 1977: 298). Echoing Descartes, Husserl states this condition as necessity: "The epoche," he says, referring to his phenomenological technique of bracketing, "creates a unique sort of philosophical solitude which is the fundamental methodical requirement for a truly radical philosophy" (1970: 184). Whether through innate ideas, or through an otherwise *a priori* categorial apparatus, rationalism founded objectivity on the given – an ideational given present to reflective contemplation – and thus upheld methodological solipsism as completely as the empiricist tradition did.

Yet suppose an epistemology denied altogether the semantic sufficiency of the given, adhering instead to a view of experience as synthetic but not synthetic *a priori*. In that case the very basis of objectivity as construed by methodological solipsism has simply collapsed. If there is still to be objective knowledge, (i.e., knowledge which is intersubjectively certifiable through randomly replicable testing), then underlying that knowledge as its condition of possibility there must exist an intersubjective framework of epistemic conventions. These conventions, in turn, rest upon the linguistic interaction of some group of persons. Since this interaction is the precondition for objectivity, it cannot be objective *in the same sense,* for the objectification of the interaction would itself presuppose a set of interactionally founded conventions, and the objectification of these would in turn presuppose another set, and so on *ad infinitum* (cf. Apel 1977: 295). Always, and inevitably, there remains a communicative residue which cannot be fully objectified – short, that is, of returning to the tenets of methodological solipsism.

We can now grasp what is so devastating about Blumer's disconnection of methodology and symbolic interactionism. It is not just that two inconsistent semantic theories are juxtaposed; rather, the problem consists in the subsumption of a social theory of knowledge under the tenets of a methodologically solipsistic epistemology. The inconsistency could hardly be more fatal to the aspirations of methodological coherence.

In our critical extensions we have already moved toward a social epistemology simply by rejecting Blumer's look-and-see empiricism, whose assumptions are, after all, necessary for the empiricist form of methodological solipsism. To put Blumer's methodology on a coherent footing, we have now to connect our revised empiricism to the interactionist view of language and linguistic interaction as essentially social. That thesis is construed along lines similar to the later Wittgenstein's notion of language-games: language is viewed as a part of social behavior (cf. Blumer 1969b: 9). In the course of this behavior, different indications are made, and with these arise different "objects" (Blumer, 1969b: 10). These objects together compose a "world" (or "worlds"), which thus contains inherently a reference to joint action and mutual interaction.

Incorporating these interactionist tenets into methodology, we approach from a different direction, and more comprehensively, the view already attained by the earlier argument into the conditions of the possibility for objectivity: symbolic interaction is a founding stratum for objectifying knowledge. What specifies epistemologically the general meaning of science as a social enterprise is – to employ Gadamer's expression – a *participatory belonging* to this stratum. Blumer, of course, acknowledges the collective nature of science (1969b: 23), but his veerings toward methodological solipsism preclude him from giving that nature adequate explication.

Science as value-laden.   From the sociality of knowledge we turn now to consider another issue: the valuational facet of science. As noted in Chapter 2, Blumer's thinking on the criteria for evaluating scientific theory underwent several changes. Its earliest phase tended to elevate prediction and control to sovereign normative status (1931: 531; 1939: 115), although other criteria, such as internal consistency, external consistency with other theories, and generality, were also admitted (1939: 112). With the ascendance of his look-and-see empiricism, Blumer stressed empirical adequacy as the decisive matter, abandoning reference to prediction and control and relegating other criteria to provisional stand-ins required by the methodical difficulties of observational verification (1940: 719). Finally, in his last phase, Blumer dropped all reference to any evaluative standard other than empirical adequacy.

Blumer's final view acknowledges only that "the free pursuit of truth, wherever it may lead, is the basis of science and scholarship" (1967a: 158). Truth itself requires no real specification of subsidiary or constitutive values because it is conceived as exclusive of these. Indeed, the inclusion of subsidiary values can only serve as a distorting factor, a source of bias, a bad grid. The thinking behind this view is, of course, look-and-see empiricism, which holds that the world, given in originary self-display, can be grasped as simply itself (i.e., objectively) only when the scientific observer is careful to subtract out all preferences and partialities which obstruct the pristine visibility of things. Values become *psychological* matters having no *logical* relationship to knowledge.

This particular marriage of empiricism and value-neutral objectivity comes to an end with the death of its dominant partner. And, as has been argued, look-and-see empiricism is indeed dead. The revised empiricism that has been delineated requires for values a different role within science. In particular, that role follows upon the slippage that has occurred in the grasp that theory has upon the world, a slippage drawing a dual locus of support in the underdetermination of theory by fact and the theory-ladenness of observation.

It is the gap between theory and the world that provides an opening in which values can be logically sited (Hesse 1978: 2). Indeed, given the inevitability of theory in science – "theory" broadly conceived as virtually coextensive with intelligibility itself – and the underdetermination of theory by fact, additional criteria besides empirical adequacy are called upon to perform a theory-founding chore. These criteria are values, whether formal considerations such as simplicity, or material ones such as preferred metaphysical schemes. Such schemes, the most abstract layers of a theory, are (at least in particular research contexts) relatively immune from empirical verification or falsification, and yet seem to figure inevitably in the very tissue of intelligibility, as epistemological rationalism has recognized as far back as Plato. Given this, it is clear that the values underlying the choice of categorial frameworks – values equivalent to preferences as to how the world *should* be – belong conceptually to the particular intelligibility the world assumes relative to a framework.[2]

When values are viewed as belonging conceptually to the enabling conditions for knowledge, then the relationship between fact and value is no longer conceived epistemologically as an *empirical* relationship between subjective phenomena (values) and objective phenomena (facts). In that sort of relationship, the only appropriate stance for the objective seeker of knowledge is indeed the bracketing of all values (other than the value of the bracketing itself). Rather, the fundamentally enabling relation of value to fact implies that the relationship between the two is of a logical character, not in the sense of a formal logic, but a transcendental one – a logic of conditions of possibility.

This view has been given considerable development in the writing of Michael Polanyi. "I want to show," he says, "that scientific passions are no mere psychological by-product, but have a logical function which contributes an indispensable element in science" (1962: 134). Polanyi distinguishes two overlapping sorts of transcendentally functional scientific values: "intellectual passions" and "conviviality." The first sort refers ultimately to a phenomenological intuition of intellectual beauty (1962: 135), which is functionally channeled into selective, inventive, and persuasive impulses (1962: 159). The second kind of value – "conviviality" – comprises the "civic coefficients" of the intellectual passions (1962: 203); these include the values underlying interpersonal association and societal organization. In Polanyi's epistemology both sorts of values are logical essentials.

We might contrast Polanyi's view of values in science – especially the civic values – with Blumer's. As we have seen, Blumer developed his methodology to where it touched critically upon the social organization of science, urging the need for professional associations to counter the threats government funding allegedly poses to social research. Yet Blumer's conception of these threats is telling: He sees them as assaults upon disinterested objectivity and therefore upon empirical adequacy. In short, these social forces intrude into the otherwise autonomous province of scientific activity, and it is the duty of professional associations to keep them out. Relegated to this function, professional associations are themselves construed as regulative bodies extrinsically related to the findings of an autonomous scientific method. Thus, even Blumer's treatment of the social organization of science remains tethered to the tenets of methodological solipsism. In contrast to this view, a social epistemology (such as Polanyi's) encompasses the *valuational* coefficient of symbolic interaction (however this coefficient may be specified) as part of its logical apparatus.

Ontological repair

Thus far our critical extensions have focused upon the epistemological side of Blumer's methodology. Now, in the remainder of this chapter, we will consider the ontological assumptions in Blumer's view of science. Here, as before, there are serious problems with Blumer's formulations, and therefore there is considerable need for repair. Our point of departure will be Blumer's own statement of his ontological standpoint.

In response to two critics, Blumer summarized his position in four theses:

1. There is a world of reality "out there" that stands over against human beings and that is capable of resisting actions toward it;

2. This world of reality becomes known to human beings *only* in the form in which it is perceived by human beings;

3. Thus, this reality changes as human beings develop new perceptions of it; and

4. The resistance of the world to perceptions of it is the test of the validity of the perceptions (Blumer, 1980: 410).

Blumer goes on to contrast his position with the views of both idealism and realism. In opposition to idealism, Blumer asserts the existence of a real world "which may not be perceived at all by human beings or which may be perceived incorrectly" (1980: 410). In opposition to realism, Blumer denies the existence of a real world having a fixed, intrinsic makeup, insisting that the real world "may change as human beings reconstruct their perceptions of it" (1980: 410). Blumer thus views his stance, which he regards as Mead's also, as a third option, departing from the traditional ontological choice of either idealism or realism.

I want to argue, in line with Blumer's critics (McPhail and Rexroat 1979: 457), that Blumer's supposed third option is in fact nothing more than an *inconsistent juxtaposition* of ontological claims. We can see this in the very theses with which Blumer delineates his stance. According to the first thesis, thought and being are not identical; this is Blumer's denial of idealism. On the basis of this denial, the fourth thesis becomes plausible, namely, that the world resists human perceptions and thus provides a test of them. Yet in the third thesis, Blumer argues that reality changes with the perception that human beings have of it. Clearly, the implication is that reality is mind-constituted, the very view denied in the first thesis. Blumer cannot seem to decide whether the world is or is not a function of human perspectives. Quite inconsistently, he vacillates between both views.

The source of Blumer's inconsistency lies in the analytic underdifferentiation of his concepts. *Discovery* of the world (theses 1 and 4) and *creation* of the world (thesis 3) cannot consistently be maintained as long as there is only one logical space within which both must occur; purely at the ontological level, the world is either given to perception *or* created by it, but not both. To maintain the discovery *and* creation theses requires a different logical space for each. More specifically, what Blumer needs is a distinction between ontology and epistemology such that his formative, creative thesis is held to the epistemological dimension, while the discovery thesis is tied to ontological matters. In other words, the *being* of the world is regarded as a real given, independent of human perspectives and therefore able to resist them. *Knowledge* of this real world, on the other hand, is dependent upon the creative formation of perspectives by human actors. This is indeed the idea conveyed in the second of Blumer's theses.

He only needs to carry through with this epistemological emphasis in his third thesis, recognizing that the reality which changes with changing perspectives is our experienced world, not the world as it is in itself.

Blumer is, of course, impeded in any designation of an active, constructive epistemology by his methodological involvement in look-and-see empiricism. Yet, as has been argued, such empiricism is not only false in itself, but inconsistent with the interactionist view of meaning and experience. Once these problems are effectively disposed of, there remains nothing to bar the proper analytic refinement of Blumer's formulation such that epistemological and ontological aspects are distinguished, thereby removing any vacillation between idealism and realism.

Having separated epistemological from ontological concerns, we need to look closely at those of Blumer's views which are *genuinely* ontological. The argument to be developed here is that, his disavowals to the contrary, Blumer's position, at least in its general purport, is fundamentally that of realism. In order to see this, we must be clear not only about the views Blumer has set forth in his writings, but also about the tenets implied in a realist ontology.

In a minimal sense, realism asserts the existence of a world independent of human thoughts and perceptions. In this sense, Blumer's position has always been realist. In his earliest published paper (1931: 517ff.) and in his last major methodological statement (1969b: 21–3) – not to mention the first thesis noted above – Blumer drew attention to the obdurately factual character of the world, its ability to resist our conceptualizations of it. Moreover, he viewed this resistance factor as a condition for the possibility of scientific inquiry (1969b: 21). Blumer's minimalist realism, then, is an overriding fact of his methodology *despite* the vacillation we have noted in his 1980 formulation.

But there is more to Blumer's ontology than minimalist realism. Analytically distinguishable from that stance is the meaning taken on by realism in its contrast with nominalism. Such realism is not entailed by minimalist realism; in Kant, to cite an instance, the latter position is conjoined with nominalism. Let us clarify these views before considering which of them best characterizes Blumer.

In the semantic–syntactic sense, something can be said to have a nature whenever its concept has a definition. For the nominalist, the nature of anything is limited to just this sense. The realist, by contrast, holds that the nature of certain class terms is *existential* as well as discursive; structures are a property of being and not just a property of our discourse about being.

In Blumer's first paper, we find an expression of this sort of realism. The scientific concept, he asserts, "does not merely suppose the existence of something which bridges perceptual experiences, but it implies that this thing has a nature or a certain character" (1931: 519). In his 1969 methodological paper, Blumer reiterated this point. Noting that the world stands over against the scientific observer, he adds that it has a nature or "character that has to be dug out and established through observation, study, and analysis" (1969b: 21–2). Throughout his writings, Blumer alludes to the "nature" of various social phenomena in a context which makes clear that he regards such nature as something there in the world to be "dug out and established" (cf. McPhail and Rexroat 1980: 421). In light of the textual evidence, the general purport of Blumer's ontology is realism in the sense of that term which contrasts with nominalism.

Yet Blumer wants to deny that he is a realist. Why so? Part of the answer lies in his view that his position presents an alternative to *both* realism and idealism. But as we have seen, Blumer's putative third option is only an inconsistent wavering between realism and idealism. Moreover, Blumer's denial is externally inconsistent with the strong realist purport actually taken in his methodological writings. Lastly, Blumer appears to shun any open avowal of realism because of some adventitious imputations he makes to that position: He seems to think that realism implies the belief in a fixed and eternal reality, without any possibility of change or emergence (cf. 1980: 410). While such a view has appeared in some historical versions of realism (e.g., Plato's), it is not inherent to realism per se.

Blumer does make one point that is of central importance. Citing some aspects of traditional realism which impaired its fruitfulness, he includes among them the belief that the character of the world consists in some ultimate form at whose discovery science aims. It is not so much that this belief is false, but the manner of its application, which renders it damaging: The tendency is to take *existing knowledge* as equivalent to knowledge of that ultimate form, thus blocking new inquiry (1969b: 23).

Blumer's caveat is a worthy warning, although it can certainly be turned against Blumer himself in those areas where he treats his own formulations as embodying immediate ontological authority. Moving beyond look-and-see empiricism with a corrected version which recognizes the necessity for super-sensible universals and acknowledges the synthetic character of experience along with the corollary of that view, the reflexivity of theory testing, we see first that the theoretic and ontological senses of the "nature" of a thing need to be carefully distinguished. Furthermore, within a tenable realism, the ontological structure of any phenomenon needs to be treated as a regulative idea, as an always tentative limiting concept. The reason for this is apparent: Being does not show itself directly, but only through the prism of human interpretations, and it is in the conflict of these various interpretations that knowledge grows and develops. In consequence, ontological authority is indefinitely postponed through the open course of inquiry.

Yet still the authority that science seeks is in the final analysis ontological. This point indicates another facet of realism, one which arises in its debate with instrumentalism. The debate hinges on two questions: Do theoretical entities exist? Are theoretical statements true (or at least candidates for being true)? The realist answers both questions in the affirmative. The instrumentalist, by contrast, holds that theoretical entities do not exist and that theoretical statements are neither true nor false, but only more or less useful calculating devices (cf. Klemke, Hollinger, and Kline 1980: 144ff.). Blumer's opposition to instrumentalism in this sense is assumed everywhere throughout his writings, though nowhere explicitly argued. His vehement insistence that theory and method must transcend any tendency toward self-enclosure to grasp the workings of the world makes sense only as a realist stance.

All in all, what makes Blumer's ontological purport one of realism, over and above his own protestations to the contrary, is the weight of the textual evidence considered in light of a properly differentiated and clarified analytic framework of concepts.

A final issue to emerge concerns the specification of Blumer's realist purport in the context of his substantive sociological formulations. What analytically separates this issue from the foregoing discussion is this: Logically, it is possible to adhere to realism (in all senses mentioned above) without becoming committed to any *specific* inventory of real universals. Realists can disagree among themselves in specific matters without for that reason ceasing to be realists. The question before us thus becomes one of inquiring whether Blumer was a *social* realist or not. We will consider this issue in the section "The Theorization of Society" in Chapter 4.

Notes

1 Within the logical apparatus at their disposal, the positivists could not subject dispositional terms (e.g., the *fragility* of glass) to full semantic reduction. Technically speaking, such terms "are not explicitly definable if the theory is to be axiomatized in first-order predicate calculus with equality" (Suppe 1977: 20).

2 One word of qualification needs to be injected here. The admission of enabling conditions that open up the world in a certain way does not imply that any particular condition is incorrigible. On the contrary, new orientations can in principle always be invented and tested against experiential consequences that arise relative to themselves *and* to other orientations. Theories are constrained by facts, though for the most part not unambiguously.

4. Methodical holism: Issues and applications

Throughout the course of Blumer's methodology, we have witnessed the persistence of methodical holism as a central theme. We also saw how Blumer's empiricism grew to override that theme, pressing Blumer to formulate his position as a methodical atomism even as that formulation clashed with his actual practice. This basic inconsistency cannot stand uncorrected.

In fact, we have already achieved a correction in our critical rejection of Blumer's look-and-see empiricism. With an alternative formulation – an empiricism which admits super-sensible universals and construes experience synthetically – we have established an orientation which provides for holism at the level of method. Indeed, methodical holism is but one aspect of theory testing viewed as a reflexive movement. The latter, generally stated, refers to the inclusion of theory, method, and data within a sphere of discourse conceived as categorial synthesis. This is to say that a common semantic framework interpenetrates all three elements and binds them together in one discursive region. Without such binding the discourse of science would fall apart into disparate elements, and it would be quite impossible to conceive data as testing theory for the simple reason that data would have no *relevance* to theory.

One example might clarify the point. Assume the statement "all swans are white" to be a theory that we would like to test empirically. Further assume that the only observation language consists of expressions such as white patches, brown patches, blue patches, green patches, etc. What happens in this situation is that, as long as the theory term "swan" is understood in the ordinary sense, our theory cannot be tested because no term in our observation language corresponds to it. Empirical testing requires an overlap between the languages of theory and observation.

Yet such overlap cannot be established through correspondence rules conceived as reduction sentences for defining theory in terms of experiential givens; the failure of positivism warns us against this possibility.

64

Rather, the language of theory is semantically emergent (i.e., nonreducible), and its overlap with observation language occurs through semantic synthesis between the two. Such an overlap accounts for the reflexivity of theory testing.

The notion of methodical holism emphasizes a certain segment of the interpenetrating semantic framework connecting theory, method, and data, namely, the theory–method segment. The explication of that segment can begin with either term and move toward the other. In the first case, the question is: What does theory imply regarding specific techniques or procedures necessary to test it? From the other direction, the question is: What does this or that technique imply regarding the theory which it would purport to test? In Chapter 2, we followed Blumer's answer to the first question as it was applied to the tenets of symbolic interactionism. In the present chapter, we will examine further his contributions to, and problems with, the implementation of methodical holism.

Public opinion and the sample survey

Blumer's discussion (1948) of the methodical problems connected with a research interest in public opinion begins with a denial that those problems are *merely* methodical. On the contrary, the "chief preoccupation" of students of public opinion, "the internal improvement of technique" (1948: 542), tends merely to lead research away from its genuine scientific responsibilities. These responsibilities converge in the goal of *discovering the world's intelligibility*. This simple formula encompasses, on the ontological side, Blumer's realism, and, on the theoretical side, his defense of the intelligibility of discourse in science.

Such intelligibility requires generic terms, and here public opinion research falls short. That research, Blumer complains, attests to an inability "to isolate 'public opinion' as an abstract or generic concept which could thereby become the focal point for the formation of a system of propositions" (1948: 542). Such an inability is manifested in the lack of effort applied toward identifying public opinion as an "object," in the absence of studies designed to test general propositions about public opinion despite the proliferation of empirical research directed toward it.

What disturbs Blumer is not so much the absence of general knowledge about public opinion as the complacency of researchers who are so bound to narrow questions of technique that they fail to pursue the genuine theoretical interest of science. In regard to the operationalist position, which justifies theory indifference by simply equating public opinion with measurements obtained through techniques, Blumer offers his standard objection that operationalism simply serves up data without rendering them meaningful (1948: 543). Whether through lazy neglect, or through the deliberate operationalist legitimation of that neglect, public opinion research fails to meet the intelligibility requirement of science.

What obviously is called for is theory-oriented research whose technical apparatus is tailored to fit the specific character of the theory being tested. For the case in point, this would entail an "independent analysis of the nature of public opinion in order to judge whether the application of . . . technique fits that nature" (1948: 542–3). Such an independent analysis must not be taken to enjoin recourse to methodical atomism, for that segmental look-and-see view of inquiry would simply obviate the need for selecting a specific method consonant with the theory to be tested by that method.

Blumer himself is confused on this point and does not escape a certain paradox. We witness it emerging, for example, in his proposed model of public opinion, which, as he tells us, was "derived partly from direct empirical observation and partly from reasonable inference" (1948: 543). The first source of derivation represents methodical atomism; the second is consistent with methodical holism. Juxtaposing the two in this manner produces, as just indicated, a paradox of prior verification: If the nature of something must already be known (through, for example, "direct empirical observation") in order for the proper methods consonant with it to be employed in testing it, and if the nature of something can only be known through tests employing consonant methods, then we are barred from entering a testing procedure which logically has the character of a closed circle.

The way out of this impasse is to settle the competing epistemological loyalties in Blumer in favor of the tenable option. This means abandoning the reductive empiricism, with its correlate of methodical atomism, for an empiricism that articulates methodical holism. By freeing the latter theme from a dissonant epistemological overlay (which is untenable anyway), we assist Blumer's thinking to reach its own truth.

An independent analysis of a subject matter for the purpose of prescribing appropriate research methods, then, should be viewed as an abductive reflection which utilizes whatever pertinent research is available to formulate a theory as to the nature of the phenomenon in question.[1] The theory prefigures the method and data which would test it, and testing, thus, is reflexive. In this way, the procedural circularity of research does not become an impenetrable closed circle.

With this logical matter behind us, we can proceed to consider the topic of public opinion. Blumer delineates the generic constitution of this topic and then attempts to ascertain whether the standard sample survey is an appropriate research tool for measuring it. Let us follow his discussion closely.

Public opinion, in Blumer's view, is essentially characterized in six features (1948: 543–6):

1. Public opinion is functionally set within a society. Its form is established through, and its function is a part of, the specific social processes at work within a given societal framework.

2. Society is not an aggregate of disparate individuals, but an organized nexus of different groups which are functionally diversified through special interests. These interests need to be viewed against the background stratification of power and prestige. Moreover, each functional group has an organization, the chief prominent feature of which is a leadership structure of some sort.

3. The various functional groups within a society have to act through the channels that are available to them (at least short of revolution). Individuals or groups who occupy strategic locations in the channels of social action will be the recipients of influence and pressure that functional groups bring to bear in pursuit of their specific interests.

4. Strategically placed individuals, when confronted with the various influences and pressures brought to bear upon them, will assess these influences and pressures in the course of arriving at decisions.

5. Public opinion is formed and expressed within the social processes described above. In its formation, public opinion derives largely from the interaction of groups, each of which is internally differentiated in matters pertinent to opinion formation (knowledge, activism, leadership, etc.). In the interaction between groups, stratified resources such as prestige, position, and influence become key factors in determining the character of the public opinion that emerges through the interaction.

The same social processes at work in the formation of public opinion are also operative in its expression. That is, various groups, differentially endowed with social resources, pursue their ends through the available channels of action. The expression of group interests occurs within these channels.

6. Given this manner of expression, public opinion properly speaking consists of the diverse views brought to the attention of strategically significant individuals (i.e., persons who have to act in response to public

opinion). Blumer's view, then, conceives public opinion as part and consequence of specific societal operations; opinion outside these operations is not, strictly speaking, public.

Against this background model of public opinion, how does the standard sample survey fare as a measuring device? It fails, says Blumer, because:

Its current sampling procedure forces a treatment of society as if society were only an aggregation of disparate individuals. Public opinion, in turn, is regarded as being a quantitative distribution of individual opinions (1948: 546).

In short, a survey based on standard sampling procedures does not tap the socially functional character of public opinion.

We can witness this shortcoming by considering a number of questions which remain unanswered in the findings of an opinion survey. Typically, persons serving as respondents are selected without regard for what groups they belong to, how well organized these groups are, the extent of their concern with an issue, their potential for social activism, their position in the stratification of society, and so on (1948: 546–7). It is these matters that strategically placed persons try to ascertain in assessing the opinions that are brought to their attention. Such a manner of assessment intimates the real mode of social efficacy for opinions, and therefore their true place in the working of an organized society. The fact that the opinion survey samples without regard to these crucial issues attests to the "inaccurate and unrealistic picture of public opinion" that it provides (1948: 547).

In Blumer's view, the problem cannot be rectified by simply adding questions to the sample survey so that it can tap the neglected areas. Rather, the root difficulty inheres in the method of sampling itself, a method which presupposes a population of discrete, standard units, some of which are gathered for study on the basis of random selection. Public opinion, as designated by Blumer, simply does not meet this presupposition; its carrying base is not an assemblage of interchangeable units, but a "complicated system of interacting parts having differential influence in the total operation" (1948: 549).

Given the disjunction between public opinion and standard sampling procedures, the appropriate research question is: What sampling technique is consonant with the theorized character of public opinion? Blumer likens this character to an organic structure, and specifies the methodical problem as how such a structure can be sampled. In order to know what is going on within the "moving organization of interconnected parts," it is necessary to dip in here and there. The problems of where to dip in, how to dip in, and how far to dip in are what I have in mind in speaking of sampling an organic structure (1948: 549).

As far as Blumer sees, the sampling problem is one whose solution remains to be found. In lieu of a solution, he offers only the suggestion for a possible line of thinking. Such a line hinges upon the formulation of a model, one which works backward from the strategic impact of opinion to the initial conditions of its inception. This model, if it could be worked out – and Blumer leaves the matter an open question – *might* permit the development of a "realistic method of sampling" (1948: 549). The hesitancy with which he expresses himself indicates his own estimation of the difficulties involved in the task.

Blumer's critical appraisal of the sample survey certainly does not imply his wholesale rejection of it. On the contrary, the fact that it fails to measure "public opinion" says nothing about its appropriateness in other research contexts. Generally, these contexts warrant the sample survey whenever their object of investigation is specifiable as an aggregate of individual units. In social research, the sample survey is thus suited to the study of such mass actions of individuals as casting ballots, buying toothpaste, reading newspapers, etc. (1948: 548–9). The success of the sample survey in consumer research, and also in election forecasting, derives, in Blumer's view, from the individual character of the actions under study.

Blumer's work on public opinion and the sample survey, to sum it up, is a case study in the exercise of methodical holism. He takes a standard research tool and interrogates it to disclose its "implicit imagery and logic" (1948: 549). These represent the point of conjunction between theory and method, the locus of an interpenetrating semantic framework. Methods always contain *substantive specifications* for the subjects they would purport to study. The methodical holist attempts to dig out these specifications in order to establish their consistency with the specifications *explicitly* posited by theory. In the following section, we will delve further into the matter of fit.

Misuse of the variable

In his 1956 presidential address to the American Sociological Society, Blumer read a paper which responded critically to a widespread and growing tendency of social research, namely, the reduction of social life to variables and their relations. Because this research format appeared on the verge of becoming a methodical norm, Blumer, always vigilant as critic of sociology, took the occasion of addressing his colleagues to challenge their methodological somnambulism. He attempted to characterize both the actual shortcomings *and* the inherent limitations of "variable analysis." We need to scrutinize his argument closely to unpack the methodological issues so densely compressed within it. As an aid in this effort, I will first expound and criticize the argument and then apply it for purposes of elucidation to two specific research studies.

Blumer begins by identifying three shortcomings that exist in the *actual practice* of variable analysis (1956: 683–5). In the first place, very little guidance is provided for the choice of variables, and the consequence is: anything goes. Variables may be simple, complex, specific, evident, imputed, doctrinaire, immediate, or constructed; they may be chosen on the basis of impressionistic appeal, through conventional usage, by consonance with a preferred technique, through adherence to some extraneous doctrine, or on the basis of "imaginative ingenuity in devising a new term" (1956: 683). The choice of variables reflects, not simply a normative anarchy, but a *failure of reflection*. And it is this failure for which Blumer takes variable analysis to task.

The point behind Blumer's objection is that research requires the guidance of theory. This requirement, seemingly so platitudinous, is not as lightly fulfilled as many researchers imagine. It encompasses thorough, careful reflection on the problem motivating the research, intensive and extensive familiarity with the empirical area under study, and comparative assessment of the different theoretical schemes that might be employed. "Current variable analysis in our field," Blumer complains,

is inclined to slight these requirements both in practice and in the training of students for practice. The scheme of variable analysis has become for too many just a handy tool to be put to immediate use (1956: 684).

As we proceed to reiterate and expand what Blumer understands by "theory," we will see why he believes the requirements of theoretical reflection have been slighted.

The second shortcoming of current variable analysis is the absence of truly generic variables. Blumer identifies three sorts of variables which purport to be generic but, in his view at least, are not. The first sort consists of those which are referentially bound to a given historical and cultural setting. The second sort consists of those sociological concepts (e.g., "social cohesion," "social interaction," etc.) that Blumer had previously described as sensitizing. The third sort consists of a special set of terms such as "sex," "age," "birth rate," and "time period" (1956: 684).

Since it is far from obvious that these sorts of variables are not generic, let us follow Blumer's reasoning on the matter.

The first sort of variable – that which stands for historically or culturally bound items – is not truly generic simply because it does not "stand directly for items of abstract human group life" (1956: 684). Blumer admits that variables of this type *are* class terms (1956: 684), and yet he still refuses to accord them the full status of genericity. Such refusal is most curious, and, in fact, untenable. We need to see why.

We first must distinguish between the *intension* and the *extension* of a concept. The former refers to those qualities or properties which compose the concept, whereas the latter signifies those instances which exemplify the concept. Blumer's failure to draw this distinction – indeed, his actual conflation of the two aspects – stood behind the insoluble semantic problem contained in the notion of the sensitizing concept. Having moved beyond that notion by opting for the clear universality of scientific concepts, Blumer is still unable to articulate formally the nature of such universality. In fact, he even retains the tendency to conflate intensionality and extensionality.

We find an expression of this tendency in his denigration of concepts that designate historically specific (i.e., extensionally bound) items. By insisting that a term, to be a universal, must have an unrestricted extension, Blumer returns to his earlier effort to found the meaning of a term on the serial presentation of its particular instances. The failure of this effort should have motivated him to distinguish clearly between intension and extension and to recognize that what characterizes a universal is not the inclusiveness of its extension, but the fact that it can function intensionally. As long as the latter condition obtains, a concept is a universal even if it has *no* empirical exemplifications.

This logical point is far from inconsequential for social research. If recognizing with Blumer that science – indeed, intelligibility itself – requires concepts (and not just proper names), we erroneously hold with him that historically bound items cannot be designated by genuine concepts, then it would follow that social research must renounce culturally and historically specific topics from its sphere of investigation.

Such, indeed, is the position toward which Blumer's view of universals drives him, although he stops short of actually embracing it. Speaking of the concept "social development," he says:

Even though this process is not a true universal, because of time and space limitations, it could still be regarded as having a common and abstract character which might be disengaged through sociological study (1966b: 8).

Thus, Blumer waffles a bit in his understanding of genericity. The corrective for this predicament lies simply in recognizing that the assayed distinction between "true universal" and class term (cf. 1956: 684) is untenable.

We might inject here that this distinction appears to be one underlying dimension (though not the only one) in Blumer's demarcation of different types of social theory. He distinguishes scientific theory proper from two other sorts: one which seeks to develop a meaningful interpretation of a specific social world, and one – "policy theory" – which analyzes a concrete situation as a basis for policy or action (1954a: 3; 1955b: 21). Yet these distinctions, at least to the extent that they derive from a faulty understanding of universals, are themselves superfluous.

At any rate – to return to Blumer's claim that variable analysis lacks generic variables – let us reassess the matter. The first sort of variable which is alleged to be nongeneric, the historically delimited variable, is falsely charged. Extensionally bound concepts can qualify as universals as long as they are in principle intensionally functional.

The third sort of allegedly nongeneric variable can be considered ahead of the second, since it differs little from the first. Blumer identifies a special set of class terms (sex, age, birth rate, and time period) which are universally applicable to human group life, and yet which appear not to function as generic variables (1956: 684). The reason for this, Blumer argues, is that:

Each has a content that is given by its particular instance of application, e.g., the birthrate in Ceylon, or the sex distribution in the State of Nebraska, or the age distribution in the City of St. Louis (1956: 684–5).

Blumer's position here seems to repeat his view concerning the first sort of variable, namely, that extensional boundedness nullifies genericity. The only difference between the first and third sorts of variables appears to be the *source* of extensional restriction: With variables of the first sort, it is the subject matter which places restrictions, whereas with the third sort, it is scientific practice which places them. Yet the source of extensional restriction is logically irrelevant to the question of genericity, and, as we have noted, universality is not nullified by extensional delimitation. So once again Blumer's argument fails to sustain its conclusion.

Turning to the second type of allegedly nongeneric variable – the sensitizing concept – we find a different underlying argument. Blumer appears to be saying that sensitizing concepts, which are intensionally vague, receive a more definite content within the context of particular research problems; the content thus varies from problem to problem, and in that sense is localized. In other words, what occurs is that a concept which is more or less vaguely understood is subjected to *intensional reduction*. The ensuing reduced concepts are themselves universals, of course, but, *relative to the original concept*, they represent partialized, particularized contents. In this manner, theory terms are not treated generically, and, reciprocally, the generic reduced terms are not treated theoretically. From this perspective, Blumer's challenge to the genericity of theory terms does in fact make sense. Of the three sorts of allegedly nongeneric variables, then, only the second is guilty as charged.

The motivating concern behind Blumer's attention to the logic of theory terms becomes visible in his discussion of the third shortcoming of variable analysis. When concepts become particularized, they become bound to a specific "here and now" referent, which is unintelligible in that the particular per se is ineffable, as Aristotle would remind us. The particular acquires communicability and intelligibility through description of its context, something variable analysis does not usually provide. Whereas it may disclose, for example, that a significant correlation exists in a certain data set between education and income, it does not convey any meaningful account of the correlation. Providing neither generic variables nor contextual description, variable analysis is but a back door admission to operationalism.

What underlies Blumer's concern with genericity is his insistence that theory should be intelligible. This view invites comparison with Norwood Hanson's (1958) position in *Patterns of Discovery*. Arguing against the causal-chain account of causation, that is, the view that causation involves only discrete events bound spatially and temporally to neighbor events similar in structure to themselves, Hanson advances the following:

'Effect' and 'cause,' so far from naming links in a queue of events, gesture towards webs of criss-crossed theoretical notions, information, and patterns of experiment. . . . The notions behind 'the cause x' and 'the effect y' are intelligible only against a pattern of theory, namely one which puts guarantees on inferences from x to y (Hanson 1958: 64).

Theory, in short, provides an intricate pattern of concepts whose interlocking character provides the explanatory feature of genuine causal linkages. By contrast, "causal-chain accounts are just plausible when we deal with fortuitous circumstances, a series of striking accidents" (Hanson 1958: 52). And what follows from the accidental character is that "we would feel little unsettlement if one occurred without the other" (1958: 65).

Blumer, no less than Hanson, is arguing against the view of theory which sees it as merely depicting random covariation, only Blumer pursues the point through a consideration of genericity. What is flawed in his argument is that it conflates two logically heterogeneous items – universals with scope conditions and intensionally reduced concepts – and fails to see that only the second of these is actually guilty of nullifying theoretical intelligibility.[2] Once this mistake is corrected, Blumer's own preference for formal theory over historically or culturally delimited theory is deprived of any foundation in the logic of universals.

A lack of guidance by theory, the use of nongeneric concepts, and an absence of ideographic description to render nongeneric terms intelligible, these are the three shortcomings that Blumer cites in the actual conduct of variable analysis. The next step in his critique is to consider the *inherent* limitations of the variable. The first of these limitations stems from the "process of interpretation or definition that goes on in human groups" (1956: 685). Blumer's explication of this claim culminates in an identification of its logical nucleus, which he then generalizes as the second inherent limitation of variable analysis. Let us attend to his discussion.

Human group life, as Blumer sees it, is chiefly a "vast interpretive process in which people, singly and collectively, guide themselves by defining" the world that is around them (1956: 686). Given the centrality of interpretation, the topic seemingly should warrant a prominent place in social research, and yet it does not, at least in research conducted as variable analysis. The usual procedure is to identify some factor presumed to operate on social life, label that factor the "independent variable," and then to test its covariation with some aspect of group life deemed a "dependent variable." For example, such research might attempt to ascertain the impact of an economic recession on the divorce rate, using, perhaps, bivariate regression analysis in which the rate of divorce is regressed on the rate of economic growth. Even a significant relationship between the two variables, Blumer would insist, overlooks the matter of decisive importance.

That matter, of course, is interpretation. The independent variable does not automatically bring certain things about; rather, it exerts an impact *only* by entering into the experience of persons, and it enters their experience only through a process of definitional appropriation. Such appropriation, functioning as an intervening mediation between the two variables, is the real source of whatever relationship happens to exist between them. Failure to acknowledge this fact can lead to false theoretical postulates through erroneously imputed universality and necessity.

Blumer draws a distinction between situations in which interpretations are fixed and those in which they are constructed. In the former case, the tendency of variable analysis to ignore the interpretive process does no real damage, at least as long as it adds a *ceteris paribus* qualification to its statement of the related variables. On the other hand, in those situations where meanings are constructed, the failure of variable analysis to consider the interpretive process renders it out of touch with the emerging forms of social interaction.

Can variable analysis incorporate the process of interpretation, considered as a formative process? Blumer's answer is a resounding "No!", and his reason is that no aspect of the process can be given the qualitative constancy required in a variable (1956: 688). An interpretation is a semantic emergent, not equivalent to the summation of the separate items which went into it. Insofar as the variable "must be set up as a distinct item with a unitary qualitative make-up" (1956: 688), it is unsuited to deal with anything, such as interpretation, not having such a makeup. The thrust of Blumer's criticism, to phrase it differently, is to caution against committing a type of what Gilbert Ryle called a category mistake.

Blumer proceeds to expand the point to include the whole of social life. Variable analysis, with its logical need for "discrete, clean-cut, and unitary" referents, tends to work with "truncated factors" which "conceal or misrepresent the actual operations in human group life" (1956: 688). These operations constitute an "intricate and inner-moving complex" (1956: 689). For illustration – to take one of Blumer's examples he considers the variable "birth control program." This variable can be given a simple and unitary indicator – for example, the number of people visiting birth control clinics – and it can be correlated with other variables. What results can have the appearance of a simple relation between discrete social factors.

Yet such an appearance, Blumer insists, is entirely misleading. In regard to the variable "birth control program," for instance, he draws attention to *some* of the "intricate and inner-moving" social factors which underlie it:

. . . the literacy of the people, the clarity of the printed information, the manner and extent of its distribution, the social position of the directors of the program and of the personnel, how the personnel act, the character of their instructional talks, the way in which people define attendance at birth control clinics, the expressed views of influential personages with reference to the program, how such personages are regarded, and the nature of the discussions among people with regard to the clinics (1956: 688).

Such factors, in sum, are indicative of a complexity which belies the view that "birth control program" is a simple and unitary phenomenon. Blumer acknowledges that various aspects of social life differ in degree of such complexity, yet he contends generally that the implicit imagery of the variable is misleading in social inquiry (1956: 689).

Having reviewed Blumer's argument as to the shortcomings and inherent limits of the variable, let us apply it, for purposes of clarification, to specific instances of research. We will examine comparatively two studies: Howard S. Becker's "Becoming a marijuana user" (1953) and James Orcutt's "Normative definitions of intoxicated states" (1978). Since these studies employ vastly different methods and yet ostensibly represent the same theory, an obvious problem arises for methodical holism's claim that method articulates theory: Can the distinctively different methodical procedures really test the same theory? It is this, the claim of methodical holism, that guides the ensuing discussion; in looking comparatively at the work of Becker and Orcutt, our interest, pursued through an illustration of Blumer's critique of the variable, centers upon the semantic aspect of the fit between theory and method.

We begin with Orcutt's study, whose methodical scheme is variable analysis, and examine it in light of Blumer's case regarding the misuse of the variable. Blumer's first allegation – that variable analysis neglects or even ignores theory – is seemingly not true in Orcutt's study. Indeed, the subtitle of the study, "A test of several sociological theories," indicates its intention to be theory-oriented research. More generally, Orcutt subscribes to the Popperian view of science as advancing through falsification of theories (Orcutt 1978: 395).

In regard to the particular cast of its theoretical perspective, Orcutt's study aligns itself with the sociological work on drug use which began with Becker's paper, "Becoming a marijuana user." Yet Orcutt's characterization of Becker's work is telling: He refers to it as theorizing, as analysis (1978: 385), with a strong implication that it does not represent empirical testing (cf. also, 1978: 395).

Actually, Becker's study relied on a series of fifty interviews (1953: 236) to abduct and test a model of social learning involved in becoming a recreational user of marijuana. Orcutt's seeming unwillingness to accord Becker's procedure the status of empirical testing suggests that Orcutt has some very definite limits on how he construes such testing. The implication is strong that those limits are set by specific techniques or formats of research (such as variable analysis). This specification of empirical testing in methodically specific and imperative forms is, of course, an instance of the methodical apriorism against which Blumer inveighed so vigorously and which he found to lie behind the "astonishing" allegation (1969b: 48) that interactionist research employing qualitative or "soft" techniques does not qualify as genuinely scientific.

At any rate, Orcutt's study gets underway as a polygamous venture: with the one hand, it embraces Becker's theoretical perspective, and, with the other, some definite notions of proper empirical testing. Since Becker's work was not constrained by the same procedural norms, the methical holist would assay a prediction of discord in Orcutt's happy polygamy; for it to survive, some adjustments must be made.

We will consider those adjustments – to return to our semantic frame of reference – as an exercise in translation. From the perspective of a logical reconstruction, Orcutt begins with two languages, one from Becker, the other from method, and attempts to bring them together in a common discourse. The language of method is granted priority, which means that its categories are to subsume Becker's. The central category in Orcutt's language of method is that of the variable; the preferred species of this category is both intensionally and extensionally of a metric character. Such preference stems from the semantic presupposition of multiple regression, the statistical analytic technique Orcutt uses. Additionally, Orcutt's language of method uses the categories "dependent" and "independent" to qualify variables according to a hierarchy of influence.

The task facing Orcutt, then, is to translate Becker's language into method language. Since Becker does not employ the category "variable," Orcutt's first move is to identify which of Becker's terms can be subsumed under this category. Becker's research sought to characterize the interpretive content of an interactional process whose outcome was a certain definition of marijuana usage. To construe this characterization in terms of variables, Orcutt divides it into two regions: the process of interaction and the outcome of that process. Next, he assigns the hierarchically qualifying categories to his translated variables such that the process of interaction becomes an "independent variable" and the outcome of the process a "dependent variable."

But the toughest part of the translation only now begins. Given the preference in Orcutt's method language, it does not suffice simply to divide Becker's model into dependent and independent regions; what is paramountly desired is a specification of those regions in such a manner that they can be subjected to an interval-ratio level of measurement. This aspect of the translation does indeed require exquisite artfulness.

Its first step is to take the interaction process, which has become an independent variable, and impute to it the category of "extent," transforming it into "the greater one's interaction with others" (Orcutt 1978: 386). In Becker's work there is no category "extent," but only a qualitatively depicted process. To connect this process with the notion of extent in such a way that interaction is translated into a variable which is both intensionally and extensionally of a metric character, Orcutt considers the intension of the concept "interaction" with an eye toward finding some aspect of it which fits a certain semantic requirement. The basis for this requirement lies in the fact that a variable which intensionally is solely metric in character does not transcend the immanence of a calculus. To transcend this immanence toward a world of things – which, after all, is the interest of empirical science – requires an intensional expansion of the variable, not just in any direction, but in one which maintains consistency with what is semantically set down in the intension of the metric component of the variable. Only on the basis of such consistency can numbers be applied realistically, and not just nominally, to things.

The consistency requirement leads Orcutt to construct his independent variable by combining (among others) a formal category, "number," and a material category, "closest friends," such that extent of interaction is measured by the question, "Of your four closest friends, how many would you say use [drug] at least once a month?" (Orcutt 1978: 387). The category "friend" is conceived as an intensional aspect of "interaction" which simultaneously maintains consistency with the semantic specification of the metric (i.e., discrete units: one friend, two friends, etc.) and retains an *oblique* reference to the qualitative character of the interaction. Orcutt's translation, thus, has moved from the qualitative concept "interaction" to a variable whose numerical extension is real rather than nominal. We will examine shortly the *cost* of this translation.

The dependent variable, the outcome of the interaction – that is, the definitional character of (in this case) marijuana as a use item – presents a tougher translation challenge. Orcutt's task is to retain, rather than intensionally reduce, an interpretive content while simultaneously providing for its interval-ratio measurement. He attempts to do this by asking his respondents to estimate the *probability* of various outcomes of drug usage, outcomes such as becoming more outgoing, less inhibited, more introspective, etc. (Orcutt 1978: 389).

One readily visible problem with this measurement is that it assumes, but makes no effort to control for, what may be described as sociological naiveté. That is, it assumes that the respondents are *ignorant* of the link between socialization and drug experience. This ignorance is, in fact, logically essential to the very meaningfulness of the study's findings, for the following reason. Variable analysis requires at least some element of conceptual independence between dependent and independent variables, for otherwise a variable is merely being correlated with itself. In Orcutt's study, this independence requirement is not met if the subjects' estimates of outcome probabilities are made on the basis of a known (or even assumed) link between outcomes and drug subculture socialization. Orcutt's failure to control for the knowledge of this link renders the findings of his study uninterpretable.

Another feature of the dependent variable warrants comment. We noted that Orcutt sought to retain an interpretive content while at the same time construct a variable measurable at the interval-ratio level. How is this possible? Orcutt's approach is to attach the content to a probability estimate. What this means is that a binary categorical outcome (i.e., either the outcome occurs or it does not) is estimated as to its *distribution* among some population, whether that population is different "average persons" using a drug, the same "average person" using the drug on different occasions, or one's own use of the drug on different occasions. Regardless of how the population is specified, one fact remains: In every instance where the estimated probability is less than one hundred percent, there will be projected cases of drug users who fail to experience a certain outcome.

Such cases do not, of course, pose any problem for a socialization theory of drug experience, which can accommodate them by specifying *qualitative* differences in drug socialization, for example, inter- and intra-subcultural differences in normative expectations. Yet the fact that these cases can be so easily accommodated raises a serious problem for Orcutt's study. Recall that the independent variable was constructed by intensionally reducing a qualitative content so as to permit an unequivocal metric measure of interaction. Without further qualitative content, however, "high interactional exposure" to a drug subculture is compatible with *any* value provided in the dependent variable. In consequence, Orcutt's study does not count as a test of a socialization theory of drug experience.

Let us return to Blumer's critique of the variable to see how it is illustrated in Orcutt's study. The first of Blumer's complaints, that variable analysis is not adequately guided by theory, appeared initially to be untrue of Orcutt's work. Yet, in an unintended and ironic turn of events, Blumer's criticism was borne out: Translating theory into method, Orcutt lost the theory and proceeded to conduct a test irrelevant to it. Orcutt's aspiration for theory-oriented research fell victim to the preemptive claims of a particular methodical scheme.

The manner in which theory got lost illustrates Blumer's second complaint. Orcutt, reducing the notion of "interaction" to a metric measure, eclipses the intension of the term; in fact, interaction per se does not appear in Orcutt's study in any shape, form, or fashion. At most, it is implied. So, in lieu of intensional articulation, the content is derived from a "here and now" context, that is, it is not generic. And this was the second of Blumer's complaints.

His third complaint, deriving from the second, is that variables, lacking intensional explication, remain unintelligible in whatever covariation they may exhibit. With a purely "here and now" content, variables may yet receive a measure of intelligible linkage in another manner, namely, through ideographic description. Such description, of course, is not found in Orcutt's study.

When we turn from the actual shortcomings to the inherent limits of variable analysis, we find that Orcutt's study presents a test case for Blumer's assessment of the matter, for Orcutt attempted to capture in terms of variables precisely what Blumer placed beyond their semantic capacity: the process of symbolic interaction. We have noted that Orcutt treats interaction by stripping away its distinctive features. In this way he constructs a measure which appears to have the discrete, clean-cut semantic constancy required in a variable. Yet, when the qualitative features of interaction are reintroduced, that constancy dissolves as the specious display of a truncated factor.

Becker's research reveals just what gets truncated. Becoming a marijuana user, as depicted in that research, involves a reciprocity of action through which a universe of common meanings imputed to the drug experience is jointly forged. Respecting the formative, volatile, reciprocal character of interaction, Becker's method is to take an outcome – in this case, using marijuana for pleasure – and to *reconstruct its history.*

In total contrast, Orcutt's approach is to take a history and try to predict its *outcome:* Interaction with experienced drug users produces (causes) certain modifications in the definitional content of experience. This *implies* a view of "interaction" which meets the constancy requirement of the variable, yet it is not at all the view of Becker. In translating the latter's theory into variables, Orcutt unwittingly substituted a different – and rather mechanical – theory of interaction for the original, or rather he would have if he had not lost theory altogether.

With his dependent variable Orcutt also faces the semantic constancy requirement; only this time, since the variable expressly comprises definitional content, that requirement is "met" differently, and more easily. Orcutt simply assumes the semantic equivalence of the responses across his sample; that is, he assumes that the numerical equivalence of outcomes estimated by different respondents is also a semantic equivalence. But this assumption, given the contextual dependence of meaning, is unwarranted. As we have already noted, without ascertaining the sociological sophistication of the respondents, we have no way of knowing whether the dependent and independent variables are logically distinct, and without this information Orcutt's findings cannot be interpreted.

In summary, a comparative examination of Becker and Orcutt in regard to the sociology of drug experience, illustrates well certain aspects of variable analysis critically cited by Blumer. If we rephrase the crux of Blumer's critique in a purely semantic frame of reference – which is preferable to his own tendency to mix indiscriminately semantic and ontological formulations, leading to the paradox of prior verification – we arrive at the following.

Variable analysis is a method language within which certain things can be said, and other things cannot be said. It is an unwarranted assumption to regard this language as the mother tongue of science. To force all theories to fit the semantic requirements of variable analysis is either to eliminate some theories by dogmatic fiat, or else unintentionally to distort them to the point of elimination (as was true of Orcutt's translation of Becker). In science it is theory which must have the upper hand in guiding research. The common discourse of theory and method, therefore, must give semantic precedence to the requirements of theory, and any translating must use its categories to subsume those of method (though without distortion).

Blumer's critique does not imply that variable analysis is without use for social research – quite the contrary. We will see that use, and some issues related to it, in the section following the next one. But first we will follow Blumer's application of his critique of variable analysis to a specific research area.

The study of mass-media effects

Research in the area of mass-media effects might raise questions such as: How do oral and visual presentations differ in their influence on retention? How do the media influence voting? How do the effects of radio differ from those of television or of newspapers? In any event, what is standard to this area of inquiry, according to Blumer (1959b: 197), is a certain research format: Some communications medium is cast as an independent variable and hypothesized the act upon a specified group of persons to produce a certain outcome, which is the dependent variable. In line with the logic of variable analysis, each factor is held to be qualitatively discrete, and the relations sought between the factors are of a stable and definitive character. Blumer applies his critique of variable analysis to challenge some underlying assumptions of media research.

First off, he notes that the various media of mass communications exhibit an internal and external variability which does not allow for the constancy and discreteness required of variables. Internally, each medium undergoes a perpetual flux in regard to its content. This indeed corresponds to the moving character of the world of which they attempt to give account. Externally, the various media are interdependent, dealing with the same happenings, taking each other into account, and responding to one another. Given the considerable extent of internal and external variation, media do not perform to the requirements of variable analysis.

Second, media research tends to identify a specified population on the basis of categories such as age, sex, education, etc., and to assume that its responsiveness to media is bound to such characteristics. What is misrepresented in this assumption are the varying ways in which persons respond to media. Presentations by the latter are filtered through a grid of malleable interests set in place by a definitional scheme. While such a scheme may be stable, it may also involve an active constructive process of interpretation, one in which the individual is guided by cues from others, particularly from reference groups (1959b: 202). Blumer underscores the importance of the collective process of definition, linking that process to the shifting character of the world in which the collective is situated (1959b: 202). The lesson, once again, is that the persons who are studied in media research do not possess the constancy required for any definitive assertion of a relationship between a communications medium and its effects.

The failure to recognize the variability of both media and persons has led media studies to propound faulty and deceptive generalizations, Blumer argues (1959b: 200–203). Yet the objection might be raised, he anticipates, that the fault lies not with the scheme of variable analysis, but only with the ineptness of its implementation. Certain remedial measures might be taken to correct this ineptness. For instance, an experiment might be conducted, using an independent variable with a fixed content presented through a discrete medium. The subjects of the experiment could be tested to detect their state of sensitivity, their interpretive frame of reference. A control group could be used. An area of behavior could be stated precisely so researchers would know exactly where to look for the effects of the medium. Any statement of research findings would express the factors involved – medium, subjects, effects – in precisely defined terms, thus avoiding empty, false generalizations.

Blumer admits that such an approach could avoid some of the problems he had identified in media studies, and yet only at great cost. That cost is the possibility of generalizing beyond the experimental setting to the real world. Blumer believes that the exacting controls involved in experimental social research create a unique situation having no analogy outside the laboratory (1959b: 204). Thus, to generalize from laboratory findings to the "crude but real world" is risky, and Blumer faults those social researchers who ignore the risk. His own view is that experimental social research is not suited to the study of real-world media effects.

Here we must pause to inject a critical word of clarification. Blumer's discussion of the limits of experimentation can easily be interpreted in a way that undermines his critique of the variable. The center of that critique, to recall it, is of a *logical* character, challenging the semantic capability of the variable for expressing qualitatively inconstant matters. His critique of experimentation, on the other hand, can be construed as purely pragmatic, that is, as invoking the hoary argument that social life is difficult to study because there are *too many* variables operating at once. In this argument variable analysis is delimited practically rather than logically, and the problem of the external validity of experimental findings can be solved by simply noting that generalizations are made not in a molar fashion from laboratory setting to real-world setting, but molecularly from variables operating in a laboratory setting to the same variables operating elsewhere, even though they may be enmeshed with other variables so as to complicate the picture of their workings. Insofar as Blumer's critique of the variable is logical in character, it precludes this solution by denying the equivalence of "variables" operating in different contexts. We will deal later with further issues involved in this discussion.

Having rejected variable analytic research on mass-media effects, Blumer's constructive challenge is to offer an alternative. His approach, in line with the tenets of methodical holism, is to begin with a model of the mass communicative process in the real world and to derive the methodical implications of that model. Chief among the features of mass communication are the following:

. . . the variant and changing character of the presentations of the media, the variant and changing character of sensitivities of people touched by the media, the process of interpretation that intervenes between the presentation and its effect, the interdependent relationship between forms of communication, and the incorporation of media, presentations, and people in a world of moving events that imparts an evolving character to each of them (1959b: 205).

From this model Blumer draws some general guidelines for media research. It should attempt to determine the sensitivities of people to media influences, examining these sensitivities diachronically and in the context of collective life. It should consider media influences in the context of other influences. It should follow the collective interpretive process in which an influence is selected, worked up, and translated into action. It should, finally, examine the various influences of media in breadth, viewing one influence in the context of the others.

Blumer acknowledges that these guidelines imply specific methodical techniques for posing problems, sampling populations, and selecting data, and that these techniques are quite different from current procedures. Yet he offers no further guidance: "The construction of an appropriate model is a hope of the future" (1959b: 206). Here, as with his examination of public opinion research, Blumer raises more questions than he answers.

Two final comments concerning Blumer's criticism of media studies will close our discussion. First, given that Blumer's earliest empirical work dealt with the impact of movies on behavior and experience (1933; Blumer and Hauser 1933), his criticism can be read as applying, in several of its major aspects, to his own work. Second, the importance Blumer places upon contextual analysis poses an interesting consequence for a formal model which comprises qualitative variance: The research interests of social scientists cannot be satisfied with the formal theory recommended by Blumer in conjunction with his understanding of "true" universals. In the final section of this chapter, we will put this insight on a logical footing, but first we will lead into it with another topic.

The theorization of society

As a preface to an examination of Blumer's theorization of society and its methodical implications, we need to reiterate and expand his view concerning the logic of theory construction. Blumer never tired of demanding that theory terms be genuinely generic in character. The following passage, though specific in the "concept" it challenges, conveys in unequivocal language the polemical flavor of Blumer's insistence:

It is no misrepresentation to say that the concept of social development has become little more than an arbitrary label with vague and inconsistent connotations and with no semblance of a generic referent. Perhaps even more notable are the obtuseness and indifference of students to this state of affairs. By and large, sociologists seem content to take the idea of social development for granted as if it had a self-evident meaning and validity. Unfortunately, this attitude immunizes them against perceiving any need of identifying the generic process or the common form of social happening that is presupposed by the general idea of social development. Feeling no such need each student is free to follow his own vague notion of social development and to "operationalize" it at will. This makes for pronounced confusion in thought and for blind effort (1966b: 4).

Inveighing against such confusion and blind effort, Blumer's work in substantive areas follows a uniform mode of criticism. It attacks a specific area for failing to treat theory terms intensionally – terms such as "attitudes" (1955a), besides the two we have already noted, "social development" (1966b) and "public opinion" (1948). Or it critically reworks the intensional character erroneously attributed to certain terms, as, for example: "social disorganization" (1937b), "morale" (1943), the "human group" (1953), "industrialization" (1960, 1964, 1965a), race relations (1955b), "collective behavior" (1959a), "industrial relations" (1947, 1954b), "fashion" (1969c), "social problems" (1971), and "social unrest" (1978).

In light of Blumer's pervasive concern with the generic requirement for theory terms, we can reconsider his understanding of universals. As previously noted, Blumer conceived "true" universals within a subject matter as those having the widest possible extension, a view which, as was argued, is at face value mistaken. Yet in Blumer's stance there is perhaps an oblique intimation of an important point concerning the categorial structure of his theory. In its intensional component, a theory term will contain a genus and a specific difference; thus, the aggregate of related terms will resemble a vertical ordering of concepts according to gradations of abstraction and a horizontal arrangement of concepts according to qualitative differences within each gradation. At the top of the ensemble is the highest material genus, what Husserl (1931: 57) termed the regional concept. This concept has the widest possible extension within the region; it is intensionally inherent in every other concept within the order. In this sense Blumer's view regarding "true" universals can be given a tenable footing by indicating the importance of the regional concept for his systematic theorizing.

A familiar sociological example of such ordering is found in the opening portion of Max Weber's *Economy and Society* (1947). Weber's elaborate framework of categories suggests, at least formally, the fulfillment of Blumer's program for theory construction. Yet Blumer did not evade his own program; although he never explicitly gathered his theoretical efforts together in a central taxonomy after the manner of Weber, he certainly could have, for a definite systematicity pervades his substantive writings. All of the critically reworked concepts mentioned above can in fact be viewed as specifications of a single regional concept. In the remainder of this section we will examine that concept and assess Blumer's methodical recommendations in light of it.

The regional concept in Blumer's sociology is "symbolic interaction," a concept which he explicates on the basis of his reading of George Herbert Mead (Blumer 1962, 1966a, 1969b). The central feature of symbolic interaction is based upon the thesis that the human person has a self, that is, has the capacity to thematize itself reflexively and to act toward itself as toward any other object. This acting-toward-self receives expression in the process of thinking, which is nothing other than making indications to oneself. It is these indications which compose the world as a meaning-structure and specify action within it. Action, thus, is a *construction,* the product of a self-indicating process, and not a release triggered mechanically by environmental stimuli.

It is important to recognize that Blumer's view of symbolic interaction is predicated on a social view of mind. Consciousness becomes an object for itself, a self-consciousness, only when it is mediated by the consciousness of another. Thus, self and other are conceptually reciprocal. With this formulation Blumer posits the ontological primacy of social relations over individual psychology: A *relation* between persons is not a property of any person considered as a discrete individual; rather, the relation is *emergent between persons.* We can see the primacy of relations in Blumer's substantive writings – for example, in his identification of different types of social relations (cf. 1954b, 1955b). Here the irreducible unit of analysis is not the individual person but differing modes of *reciprocity* between persons – for example, power relations, codified relations, and sympathetic relations (1954b: 233). Insofar as Blumer maintains the ontological primacy of relations, he is a social realist, asserting the existence of that distinctly social universal embodied in the emergent phenomenon of the relation. Social nominalism, by contrast to this view, holds that only individual persons and their characteristics are real. We will see shortly that Blumer was not entirely free of such nominalist tendencies.

Within the context of his relational mode of thinking, Blumer goes on to speak more particularly concerning his view of society. Mutual action, or interaction, requires the fitting together of individual lines of action. Each participant takes the other into account and so orients his or her action according to the interpretation placed upon the other. This process of mutual aligning, Blumer states, "is the fundamental way in which group action takes place in human society" (1962: 184). Indeed, his claim is stronger, that the ongoing process of the interaction is the "essence of society" (1966a: 544). He recognizes clearly how this view departs from other sociological approaches to the topic, and seeks to underscore the contrast.

Typically, according to Blumer (e.g., 1962: 184ff.), the sociological theorization of society omits any reference to interaction as an ongoing, interpretive construction and views it exclusively as a result of the play of various social forces, as for example, systems, institutions, roles, norms, and so on. In this way of thinking the actor is a neutral medium through which society expresses itself. Rejecting this view does not imply, as Blumer is careful to point out, a rejection of social structure per se; indeed, "such a position would be ridiculous" (1966a: 547). "There are such matters," Blumer asserts,

as social roles, status positions, rank orders, bureaucratic organizations, relations between institutions, differential authority arrangements, social codes, norms, values, and the like. And they are very important. But their importance does not lie in an alleged determination of action nor in an alleged existence as parts of a self-operating societal system. Instead, they are important only as they enter into the process of interpretation and definition out of which joint actions are formed (1966a: 547).

Blumer's position on the status of social structure is subtle, and needs to be interpreted carefully to avoid misunderstanding. The various factors comprised by the notion of social structure are not, for Blumer, self-subsistent entities, but rather *products* of human interaction. Moreover, these products – congealed outcomes – do not mechanically determine future interaction, but they do affect it in two ways: by shaping the situations in which people act and by supplying fixed sets of symbols for the interpretive process (1962: 190). The extent of these effects is socially variable; Blumer contends that structure exerts more of an impact in stabilized societies that in the shifting movements of modern societies (1962: 190).

The truth of Blumer's theorization of society is that it wants to be dialectical. On the one side, though he denies that social structure *determines* action, Blumer allows that it *affects* action (1962: 190). Conversely, action produces social structure. Blumer's view, in sum, is such as to suggest a relational unity undergoing diremption into subsistent moments whose distinction is subsequently negated.

But Blumer never quite fixes upon this dialectical manner of formulating social structure. He wavers between some vague imagery of unity, such as depicting the process of public opinion as an inner-moving organic structure (1948: 549), and a tendency to allow the constitutive moments to fall apart in separateness. Wavering between unity and difference, Blumer fails to exploit the fertile possibility of unity-in-difference, or difference-in-unity, characteristic of dialectical thinking.

The separation of theoretical moments begins where Blumer acknowledges the existence, and even importance, of areas of social life which are not mediated by the interpretive process (1956: 689). One such area would be, presumably, nonsymbolic interaction, a form of social relationship given considerable weight in Blumer's early theory (cf. 1936), though later he grants it mention more than emphasis (cf. 1969b: 8–9). Once the separation of moments has been made, social life comes to be construed atomistically (i.e., as occurring in separate and related compartments, or levels, or segments).

From an atomized view of social life, the next step is to derive certain methodical implications; in the case of symbolic interactionism, those implications would follow upon the subjectivization of meaning: Social research would be enjoined to focus exclusively upon the perspective of the actor, neglecting the study of broad-based situational factors. The methodical factor, in short, would derive from the reintroduced opposition of subject and object.

The wavering in the formal structure of his formulations drives Blumer perilously close to the progression outlined above. His methodical admonitions, particularly in the polemically fanned formulations of the 1969 paper, invite a subjectivist, nominalist misinterpretation of the interactionist position. Moreover, the injunction for research to make a "direct examination" of the social world, with attention directed to the meanings given that world by its participants, departs from an earlier position Blumer had taken in his critique of the variable (1956). There he had recognized proper and useful applications of variable analysis in two specific areas of social research: in aspects of social life not mediated by interpretation, and in stabilized patterns of interpretive interaction (1956: 689). The 1969 paper, in its exclusive focus on "direct examination," makes no brief for these uses.

The entire problem with Blumer's methodical recommendations can be epitomized in the fact that they did not, and indeed could not, provide the basis for his own substantive explorations in areas such as industrial relations, race relations, and industrialization. And yet the work in these areas is hardly beyond the interactionist pale. The upshot of this fact is that Blumer's methodical pronouncements are not adequate derivations, as recognized in the provisions of methodical holism, of interactionist theory. The inadequacy stems, in part, from the problem we have noted in Blumer's theory, namely, its slippage into a undialectical formal structure. Yet this tendency is exacerbated by another facet of Blumer's thinking, the look-and-see empiricism, with its privileged ranking of separate and discrete immediacies. In the next section we will look further at the implications of a dialectical model for interactionist research.

One final problem needs to be mentioned in conjunction with the formal structure of Blumer's theory. In his critique of variable analysis, Blumer contended that the inherent limits of this mode of research were set by the qualitative inconstancy of the factors merging in the vortex of social action, especially by the fact of qualitative *emergence*. Yet, the manner in which such emergence is conceived raises a pivotal issue for social research. If, under a nondialectical bifurcation of self and society, qualitative emergence is sited within subjectivity as a prerogative of unmotivated spontaneity, then not just variable analysis but *any* mode of social research is rendered problematic, apparently becoming limited to an historical reconstruction of action. Without order within process, process admits of no knowledge.

Blumer does not appear to restrict social research to historical reconstruction; on the contrary, he himself makes probabilistic predictions of social trends for the proximate future (see, for example, 1965b). And yet his theoretical basis for predictions remains unclarified. Blumer's hesitancy in regard to the formal structure of his theory raises some important methodological issues which he does not pursue. A dialectical model just might provide for the order within process which he sociology seems to require.

Blumer versus Erving Goffman

In 1972, Blumer published a review of Goffman's *Relations in Public* (1971) which steered the discussion beyond the specifics of that one work toward a consideration of some general issues in Goffman's sociology. Since Blumer's review contains – though only in a covered-over fashion – some points of decisive methodological significance, we will first consider what Blumer says and then interpretively excavate its hidden import.

As might be expected, Blumer is far from being solely critical of Goffman's work; on the contrary, he commends two of its features (1972: 51–2). In the first place, according to Blumer, Goffman's perceptiveness in digging out, and establishing the social significance of, "small" matters involved in face-to-face relations, constitutes in itself a significant contribution to social research. Goffman, indeed, has forced social scientists to attend to matters which they had previously failed to consider seriously – or even to apprehend at all.

The second word of approbation centers on Goffman's method. Here Blumer takes up one of his favorite themes, the opposition to methodical apriorism, and couches it polemically. By contrast to those social scientists who slavishly adhere to fixed procedures enjoined by a hollow notion of scientificity, Goffman is a free spirit. In the manner of a true scientific pioneer, Blumer commends:

> he is ever ready to probe around in fresh directions in place of forcing his investigation into the fixed protocol so frequently demanded in contemporary social research. Fortunately, his interests are in untangling the empirical world rather than in paying obeisance to some sanctified scheme for doing so. Through the use of choice accounts of human experience he cuts through to important observations that are not yielded by hosts of stylized findings (1972: 52).

Yet the undeniable merits of Goffman's work are conjoined, in Blumer's view, with some weaknesses. Generally stated, Blumer's criticism is that Goffman's sociology deals with a truncated subject matter. Blumer specifies three areas in which the alleged truncation occurs.

The first is coextensive with the focus of Goffman's work, that is, the "area of human group life that is constituted by face-to-face meetings and association" (1972: 51). Goffman believes that this area is, for analytic purposes, an object domain in its own right, having a distinctive structure which research can disclose. Blumer questions whether this assumption is realistic, that is, whether face-to-face association can be treated independently of the broader social context of organized groups and institutions. Unless and until Goffman establishes empirically the analytic separability of his domain of research, Blumer argues, that research is founded upon a question-begging premise.

The second area of alleged truncation lies in the content of face-to-face association. Blumer complains that Goffman reduces the "natural breadth" of social interaction to a single thin strand, namely, the actors' concern to create and sustain a certain impression in the eyes of others. Such a restriction has important implications. Essentially, it ignores what the actors are doing, their "business in hand," which, according to Blumer, is precisely what "initiates and sustains face-to-face association" (1972: 52). Concerned only with personal interadjustment, Goffman diverts attention from the "true nature" of interaction: "the fitting together of the respective acts of the participants as they endeavor to do what is called for in their group or joint action" (1972: 52).

Concomitant with the misrepresentation of interaction is another problem, Blumer asserts, and that is the distortion of self-interaction. It is simply not true, he insists, that the predominant mode of self-awareness consists in a self-presentational concern. "People in association," he says, "just do not go around with their attention constantly focused on how they are being regarded and on how they can influence the way in which they are regarded" (1972: 52). Rather, the span of awareness – awareness of both self and of other – falls upon the "business in hand," the formation of joint action through the construction of individual lines of action.

The third alleged truncation in Goffman's sociology – or at least in *Relations in Public,* perhaps also elsewhere (cf. 1972:53) – consists in its exclusive concern with *patterned forms* of interaction. To consider these forms only in a synchronic analysis, without attending to the diachronic movement in which they are constructed and in which they may be altered or even cast aside, is to depict a purely static world. Blumer views such a world as, at best, a partial, and temporary, truth.

These, then, are the three criticisms Blumer directs to Goffman's sociology. Of the three, it is the second that he regards as the most decisive and profound (cf. 1972: 52); consequently, that criticism becomes our best clue for disclosing the theoretical and methodological issues covertly at work in Blumer's thinking. These issues have in fact already appeared in our earlier discussion; now we have only to make apparent their function as unthematized horizon within which Blumer's critique of Goffman takes shape.

Substantively, Blumer faults Goffman for misrepresenting the "natural content" of face-to-face association, a content which, for Blumer, comprises the various intentions to act which are operative within a social setting (1972: 53). Interactionist research is thus directed toward grasping what is subjectively intended by the actor; methodically, this occurs through "taking the role" of the other, imaginatively entering into the perspective which instigates and guides the other in acting (cf. 1969b: 16).

What is significant in this is, first, the manner in which it situates social meaning within *intentions* that are freely engendered by particular subjects. These subjects, indeed, seem to enjoy a semantic sovereignty, an epistemic privilege which arises from something like Vico's identification of producer and knower. This treatment of the actor attests to what was indicated in the previous section: In the formal structure of his theory, Blumer has not freed himself from the undialectical bifurcation of subject and object, and in consequence tends to push symbolic interactionism into a theoretically subjectivist posture.

The second issue of importance in the critique of Goffman is methodical: Blumer wants research to reproduce the actors' intentions at work in a social setting. Whereas actors construct meanings, the researcher simply grasps them as self-subsistent givens. Here we witness the interpretive analog of look-and-see empiricism, representing as it does the errant disconnection of interactionist theory and methodology proper.

In order to repair Blumer's perception of Goffman's sociology, we must correct the two errors just stated. That is, we need to reestablish dialectic at the level of the subject and to reconnect symbolic interactionism and methodology. These tasks are two only in appearance; in fact they are one, for the reabsorption of interactionist theory by methodology involves no effort but only the avoidance of a spurious duplication of effort, the subsumption of a dialectical framework under a purely receptive view of knowledge. The dialectic at the level of the subject is simultaneously methodological; we have only to draw its methodical consequences. In the remainder of this section we will consider, against Blumer, a dialectical framework for a sociology which is purely interpretive, and then reconsider Goffman in light of that framework.

Our point of departure is provided by Habermas's critical appropriation of Wilhelm Dilthey's hermeneutics (Habermas 1971: 140–86). For Dilthey the logic of the *Geisteswissenschaften* is centered upon the relation of experience, expression, and understanding. Habermas finds several errors in Dilthey's handling of this triad, but indicates that in one area – the explication of autobiography – Dilthey has identified the major elements for developing a suitable model. The distinctive advantage of autobiography for a methodology of interpretation is that autobiography elevates to articulate form the manner in which everyday consciousness labors to cope with life, a labor which works as follows.

An individual life history is an integrated unity of experiences. This unity rests upon the identity of an ego and the articulation of a meaning or significance. The identity of the ego defines itself in the dimension of time as the synthesis of ever-receding experiences; it creates the continuity of life-historical unity in the flux of psychic events. The sustained ego identity allows the overcoming of the continual disintegration of life in the stream of time. What constitutes this sustained identity is the perpetuated simultaneity of a system of reference to which individual life-experiences relate as to a whole. This system of reference is an interpretive framework through which all past events are retrospectively integrated into a life unity. The image of life history which Dilthey presents is that of a self-formative process in which ego identity is constituted as the overcoming of the continual decay of identity.

The self-formative process of an individual requires symbols (i.e., language) that logically is never private but always involves intersubjective semantic validity. The methodologically significant feature of a language community is that *individuated* persons communicate within it. The general semantic validities of language constitute a reciprocal identification of persons who, nevertheless, within language, preserve their nonidentity. General and particular exist not in abstract opposition but in a movement of dialectical mediation.

Self-formation, then, occurs on both the "vertical" level of integrating particular life experiences with an autobiographical frame of reference, and the "horizontal" level of individuating persons within a language. Both levels involve a dialectic of whole (or general) and parts (or particulars). This double dialectic characterizes the "community of life unities," which Dilthey regards as the objective framework of the cultural sciences.

The object of hermeneutic understanding – what Dilthey calls significance – embodies the dialectic of general and particular. Neither aspect can be eliminated. Without the general semantic validities of language, we have only ineffably singular experiences, and intersubjective understanding becomes impossible. Without the particularization of discrete life contexts, meaning is standardized and transparent, rendering hermeneutic interpretation unnecessary. Dialogic understanding, as Habermas so aptly puts it, "moves halfway between monologue and the impossibility of linguistic communication at all" (1971: 164).

Yet the dialectical structure of the objects of hermeneutic understanding seems at first glance to be impossible. How, after all, can general and particular be synthesized in such a way as to allow for the expression of singular experiences in general terms? The answer lies in the special capacity of ordinary language.

Communication in the general symbols of language, as well as action predicated upon general norms, becomes singularized by the circumstances of their occurrence, namely, speaking and acting by a particular person at a particular time in a particular manner, and so on. The particular interpenetrates the general but can never be fully and directly taken up into it; always a gap remains between situation and linguistic object- ivation. This gap must be closed by the interpreter.

Closing the gap becomes conceivable when we consider that speech, action, and experiential expression require the interpretive supplementa- tion of the verbal with the nonverbal. It is this special kind of reflexivity which constitutes the dialectical synthesis of general and particular in the objects of interpretation. The task of hermeneutics is to decipher the self- understanding of cultural life, this self-understanding being itself based upon the reflexive relation of language and practice.

The special nature of the objects of interpretation justifies the circular- ity of hermeneutic methods. This circularity is not vicious; it would be- come so were hermeneutic objects to be either purely symbolic (i.e., ex- haustively constituted by the rules of a metalanguage) or purely factual (given as the thatness of experience). Since they are both symbolic and factual, interpretation must simultaneously decode its objects and test it- self against them in a procedure Habermas calls quasi-inductive. The her- meneutic circle, then, is required by the conjunction of symbol and fact, or, to say the same thing differently, by the conjunction of language and practice, in the objects of interpretive interest.

Hermeneutic methods are warranted by hermeneutic objects, which in turn refer back to what Dilthey called the "community of life unities." In- deed, hermeneutic objects are inconceivable apart from this community. And not only does hermeneutic understanding depend upon a language community; it reproduces the conditions which make such a community possible. For intersubjectivity, as Habermas describes it, exists as a kind of brokenness (1977: 353); the individuated moments of language threaten to sunder its communicatively necessary generality. In consequence, "the brokenness of intersubjectivity renders the continuous coordination of views in a common schema a permanent task" (1977: 355). Habermas's di- alectical framework has provided a formal basis for what in Blumer is only factual: the continuous construction of symbolic interaction.

Moreover, the framework allows us to bring to fruition Blumer's cri- tique of the variable. The qualitative inconstancy which sets the insupera- ble limit for variable analysis led Blumer, as we saw in the case of media studies, to direct research toward contextual consideration. Now we grasp that this direction is founded upon the dialectic of general and par- ticular, with interpretive social research necessarily functioning as a par- ticipating moment in the movement of mediation. Such mediation alters the framework which Blumer sets for theory construction: A hierarchically ordered logic of classes is not serviceable for interpretive inquiry; at best, it can provide a *post factum* arrangement of interpretations. Blumer never expressly drew this conclusion, but it is implicit in his critique of the variable.

Before applying to Goffman the dialectical framework which Habermas adopts and adapts from Dilthey, we must add one supplementary feature. What motivates this supplementation is a certain limiting aspect of Habermas's construal of hermeneutics, an aspect associated with the boundary he sets for its functioning. Habermas views hermeneutic understanding as primordially situated within a relationship of participatory belonging to a tradition. Methodical social research, on the other hand, is founded upon distanciation, and is therefore heterogeneous with the hermeneutic phenomenon. That phenomenon is tradition bound and tradition limited; it "comes up against walls of the traditional framework from the inside, as it were" (1977: 360). Critique of distortions coextensive with tradition itself, therefore, must occur outside hermeneutics through a "controlled distantiation" employing "empirical–analytic" procedures to generate knowledge which is then fed back self-reflectively into the dialogic encounter.

An alternative suggestion for hermeneutics is provided by Ricoeur. What is common to both Habermas and Gadamer – despite their important differences – is, in Ricoeur's view (1973), the tendency to view hermeneutics within the dichotomous *opposition* of participatory belonging and distanciation. Ricoeur wants to replace the opposition with a dialectic: Within a philosophical anthropology which centers human being upon historicity, distanciation is a constituent moment; as Ricoeur puts it, "a *consciousness exposed to the efficacy of history* can understand only under the condition of distance" (1974: 244). Participatory belonging to a tradition, which for Ricoeur as much as for Gadamer or Habermas is the originary condition for understanding, is thus a belonging-through-distance. If the critical moment, founded on distance, is never absolute, is always conjoined to a belonging, is can nevertheless attain a "relative autonomy" (1974b: 243).

Ricoeur's hermeneutics, then, is formulated with the express intention of being a *critical* hermeneutics. Accordingly, much of its attention is focused upon the founding factor of distanciation. Ricoeur provides, as it were, a cartography of distanciation within the objects of hermeneutic interest, beginning with the protodistanciation of oral discourse (1975: 132–6) and culminating in the paradigmatic case of distanciation within communication, the text (1975: 131), with attendant recognition of the textuality of action (1971).

Beside Habermas's rendering of Dilthey, Ricoeur's formulations should not be viewed as disjunctive, but as supplementary amendments. For example, the protodistanciation of oral discourse draws upon the same basic insight which in Habermas is expressed as the capacity – indeed, necessity – of ordinary language to function reflexively as its own metalanguage. The difference here between Habermas and Ricoeur is that the latter recognizes the moment of distanciation within this reflexivity, and thus provides the basis for a critical interpretation.

Let us apply the critical dialectical framework borrowed from Habermas and Ricoeur to a reading of Goffman, with the aim not simply of construing him in a non-Blumerian fashion, but of showing how a correction of Blumer's mistakes opens up a very different perspective. Since Blumer's chief criticism of Goffman's sociology centers upon its dramaturgical facet, we will turn to the *locus classicus* of that facet, *The Presentation of Self in Everyday Life* (Goffman 1959), and consider its methodical structure along with the methodological import of that structure.

Formally considered, the dramaturgical perspective comprises two analytic categories: an *interpretans,* or that which interprets, and an *interpretandum,* or that which is interpreted. Materially, the central concept of the *interpretans* is "performance," which is used, as in everyday discourse, to signify a certain intentional activity which articulates social relationships within a specific equipmental contexture. The other concepts of the *interpretans* are taken from the established lexicon of the performance or are chosen to articulate further that lexicon beyond the ready-to-hand expressions of general cultural usage. In any case, the *interpretans* has a closely crafted semantic structure, something which is not true of the *interpretandum.* The latter, considered solely in itself, has no particular structure; it comprises a wide array of everyday experiences, settings, situations, and actions. The point of interpretation is to subsume the *interpretandum* under the *interpretans* and thereby impart to it the structure, the intelligibility, which lies in the *interpretans.*

The *relationship* between *interpretans* and *interpretandum,* materially considered, is the methodological nucleus of dramaturgical sociology. The first moment of this relationship is synecdochic in character. The *interpretans,* which posits performance as an intentional activity, subsumes an array of items constituted by, for the most part, nonperformance intentionalities. In brief, the part is used to express the whole. Goffman, of course, is fully in command of this fact, as we see in his delineation of the modes of consciousness within the *interpretandum* viewed from the perspective of performance:

Sometimes the individual will act in a thoroughly calculating manner, expressing himself in a given way solely in order to give the kind of impression to others that is likely to evoke from them a specific response he is concerned to obtain. Sometimes the individual will be calculating in his activity but be relatively unaware that this is the case. Sometimes he will intentionally and consciously express himself in a given way, but chiefly because the tradition of his group or social status requires this kind of expression and not because of any particular response (other than vague acceptance or approval) that is likely to be evoked from those impressed by the expression. Sometimes the traditions of an individual's role will lead him to give a well-designed impression of a particular kind and yet he may be neither consciously nor unconsciously disposed to create such an impression (1959: 6).

What divides Blumer and Goffman is precisely this use of synecdoche. For Blumer, the synecdochic character of the relationship between modes of consciousness in dramaturgy's *interpretans* and its *interpretandum* transforms interpretation into misrepresentation: The "natural content" of everyday consciousness is subverted, or at best caricatured. And Blumer is, of course, completely correct, but only within a methodological framework which regards conscious intentionalities as an originary ground available to research in simple immediacy. Once that framework is shaken, a new view of dramaturgy opens up.

Goffman recognizes well the specious credentials of immediacy. Though he does not, in the manner of Habermas, couch his reservations in the form of a logic of interpretation, his formulations are easily assimilated into such form. Habermas, to recall, regards the individuation of meaning as involving a diremption of general semantic validities into discrete life contexts; interpretation restores the general by using the natural reflexivity of ordinary language as a guide for grasping the individual. Goffman is attuned to this reflexivity and, in fact, gives it a prominent function within the dramaturgical perspective. He distinguishes between "expressions given" and "expressions given off" (1959: 2), the former involving symbolic communication and the latter, symptomatic expressiveness – and then accords specific priority to the latter. Interpretation, for him, does not involve a reproductive apprehending of immediate intentions, but an intervention that attempts to restore dirempted meanings given in the distance.

Blumer's objection to the synecdochic relationship between dramaturgy's *interpretans* and its *interpretandum* is for Goffman, then, no serious matter. True, the synecdochic relationship is not serviceable for doing interpretation since, in drawing *interpretans* and *interpretandum* together at only a single point of intersection, it heightens the tension between their nonintersected areas. Synecdoche, just as Blumer complains, issues in a repulsion of factors, and it must be overcome if the *interpretans* is to subsume the *interpretandum*. Blumer wants to overcome synecdoche simply by rejecting it; Goffman, by dialectically supplementing it with another interpretive move.

That move is, of course, the use of metaphor to draw together the repulsed segments of the *interpretans* and *interpretandum*. Metaphor itself is a purely dialectical function of language, simultaneously affirming and negating the heterogeneity of its constituent elements. The illuminative force of metaphor is the implosion of difference. Goffman's use of synedoche, heightening as it does the nonidentity of *interpretans* and *interpretandum*, is thus a strategic necessity for harnessing the force of metaphor.

We can envision this by surmising how *The Presentation of Self* might have looked had it limited its purview to areas of intentional impression management. The connection by metaphor of the theatrical lexicon and everyday terms would then merely extend everyday vocabulary without in any way illuminating its character as action. In a word, the dramaturgical perspective would have virtually no disclosive function, no use in reconstructing perception of the familiar. It would be trite beyond redemption. Goffman avoids this outcome by employing synecdoche to set up the difference which metaphor implodes.

It is metaphor, then, that binds *interpretans* and *interpretandum* to constitute an interpretation. The moment of immediacy, synecdochically founded, is negated in the mediation of metaphor. In substantive terms, this mediation has a decisive significance, for it introduces a critique of everyday consciousness. In negating the synecdochic distance between this consciousness and the intentionalities of performance, metaphor confronts everyday consciousness with its own theatricality. Since that theatricality is, in simple immediacy, largely unacknowledged, metaphor instates to consciousness its disowned involvements.

The idea of unacknowledged intentions, so pivotal to the disclosive effect of the dramaturgical framework, suggests a mode of consciousness that Jean-Paul Sartre has depicted as *la mauvaise foi,* or bad faith. As Sartre describes it, bad faith

has in appearance the structure of falsehood. Only what changes everything is the fact that in bad faith it is from myself that I am hiding the truth. Thus the duality of the deceiver and the deceived does not exist here. Bad faith on the contrary implies the unity of a *single* consciousness (1956: 49).

Unmasking the unacknowledged intentions constitutive of bad faith is inherent to the dramaturgical framework, established by the direction of its synecdoche. The *interpretans,* comprising an intentional structure, subsumes the everyday intentions and thus dissolves them in stark transparency. This, indeed, is the moment of recognition, of insight, impelled by the undeniable fascination of consciousness with itself. Its tricks, which it knew all along, are paraded before it, and bad faith is instantly transformed into a cynicism amused by its own slyness.

The critical face of dramaturgy appears visibly near the end of Goffman's book. "Our activity, then," he informs us,

is largely concerned with moral matters, but as performers we do not have a moral concern with them. As performers we are merchants of morality (1959: 148).

Such is Goffman's verdict, and it resonates in the toppling of a hollow immediacy. The appropriation of his text is, then – as Ricoeur would put it – the ego's divestiture of itself (1981a: 191), which is simultaneously the investiture of enhanced lucidity.

The dramaturgical perspective can thus be viewed within a methodological framework quite different from the one posited by Blumer. The general validities of language, becoming individuated, undergo diremption. It is here, as Ricoeur has argued, that distanciation enters into participatory belonging, not as its abstract negation, but as its dialectical counterpart. Interpretation intervenes to restore language from its diremption while lifting it critically beyond its present reaches.

This methodological framework offers interpretive sociology a way out of the subjectivism into which Blumer, perhaps unwittingly, tends to lead it. In place of the subject as an originary center having inviolable semantic sovereignty, there appears neither "subject" nor "object," but only the unity of a moving circuit of mediations. Within this circuit, critical sociology can intervene immanently to alter its motion.

Notes

1 Cf. Peirce (1932):

An originary Argument, or *Abduction,* is an argument which presents facts in its Premiss which present a similarity to the fact stated in the Conclusion, but which would perfectly well be true without the latter being so, much more without its being recognized; so that we are not led to assert the Conclusion positively but are inclined toward admitting it as representing a fact of which the facts of the Premiss constitute as *Icon.*

More simply, Peirce identifies abduction as:

. . . where we find some very curious circumstance, which would be explained by the supposition that it was the case of a certain general rule, and thereupon adopt that supposition (1932: 375).

An example Peirce gives (1932: 53) is an episode from the work of Kepler: Trying to fit the observed longitudes of Mars with an orbit, Kepler noted that these longitudes were such as would be if Mars moved in an ellipse. This insight *inclined* him to the view that the orbit was an ellipse, although not conclusively: Further testing was needed to determine whether predictions based on this hypothesis were verified or not. In this sense, abduction is the "probational adoption of the hypothesis" (1932: 54).

2 In regard to particularization of content, what occurs in the case of extensional reduction lends itself to a different sort of mistake from that stemming from the particularization found in intensional reduction. With extensional reduction, "particularization" of content implies the setting of scope conditions which, unless they are explicitly recognized, can give rise to bogus generalizations, that is, generalizations making claims outside the established scope of the concept. But this mistake does not imply the sort of unintelligibility that arises with intensional reduction.

Bibliography

Works by Herbert Blumer

1928 *Method in Social Psychology.* Unpublished Ph.D. dissertation, University of Chicago.

1931 "Science without concepts." *American Journal of Sociology* 36: 515–33.

1933 *Movies and Conduct.* New York: Macmillan.

1933 (with Philip M. Hauser) *Movies, Delinquency, and Crime.* New York: Macmillan.

1936 "Social attitudes and non-symbolic interaction." *Journal of Educational Psychology* 9: 515–23.

1937a "Social psychology." In Emerson P. Schmidt (ed.), *Man and Society.* New York: Prentice-Hall, pp. 144–98.

1937b "Social disorganization and individual disorganization." *American Journal of Sociology* 42: 871–7.

1939 *Critiques of Research in the Social Sciences: I. An Appraisal of Thomas and Znaniecki's* The Polish Peasant in Europe and America. New York: Social Science Research Council.

1940 "The problem of the concept in social psychology." *American Journal of Sociology* 45: 707–719.

1943 "Morāle." In William F. Ogburn (ed.), *American Society in Wartime.* Chicago: Chicago University Press, pp. 207–231.

1947 "Sociological theory in industrial relations." *American Sociological Review* 12: 271–8.

1948 "Public opinion and public opinion polling." *American Sociological Review* 13: 542–54.

1953 "Psychological import of the human group." In Muzafer Sherif and M.O. Wilson (eds.), *Group Relations at the Crossroads.* New York: Harper and Brothers, pp. 185–202.

1954a "What is wrong with social theory?" *American Sociological Review* 19: 3–10.

1954b "Social structure and power conflict." In A. Kornhauser, R. Dubin, and A. Ross (eds.), *Industrial Conflict.* New York: McGraw Hill, pp. 232–9.

1955a "Attitudes and the social act." *Social Problems* 3: 59–65.

1955b "Reflections on theory of race relations." In Andrew W. Lind (ed.), *Race Relations in World Perspective.* Honolulu: University of Hawaii Press, pp. 3–21.

1956 "Sociological analysis and the 'variable'." *American Sociological Review* 21: 683–90.

1959a "Collective behavior." In Joseph B. Gittler (ed.), *Review of Sociology: Analysis of a Decade.* New York: John Wiley, pp. 127–58.

1959b "Suggestions for the study of mass-media effects." In Eugene Burdick and Arthur

J. Brodbeck (eds.), *American Voting Behavior*. Glencoe, Ill.: Free Press, pp. 197–208.

1960   "Early industrialization and the laboring class." *Sociological Quarterly* 1: 5–14.

1962   "Society as symbolic interaction." In Arnold Rose (ed.), *Human Behavior and Social Processes*. Boston: Houghton Mifflin, pp. 179–92.

1964   "Industrialization and the traditional order." *Sociology and Social Research* 48: 129–38.

1965a   "Industrialization and race relations." In Guy Hunter (ed.), *Industrialization and Race Relations*. Oxford: Oxford University Press, pp. 220–53.

1965b   "The future of the color line." In John Mckinney and Edgar T. Thompson (eds.), *The South in Continuity and Change*. Durham, N.C.: Duke University Press.

1966a   "Sociological implications of the thought of George Herbert Mead." *American Journal of Sociology* 71: 535–48.

1966b   "The idea of social development." In *Studies in Comparative International Development*, Vol. II. St Louis: Social Science Institute, Washington University, pp. 3–11.

1966c   "Foreword." In Severyn T. Bruyn, *The Human Perspective in Sociology*. Englewood Cliffs, N.J.: Prentice-Hall.

1967a   "Threats from agency-determined research: The case of Camelot." In Irving Louis Horowitz (ed.), *The Rise and Fall of Project Camelot*. Cambridge, Mass.: MIT Press, pp. 153–74.

1967b   "Reply to Woelfel, Stone, and Farberman." *American Journal of Sociology* 72: 411–12.

1969a   "Preface." In *Symbolic Interactionism*. Englewood Cliffs, N.J.: Prentice-Hall.

1969b   "The methodological position of symbolic interactionism." In *Symbolic Interactionism*. Englewood Cliffs, N.J.: Prentice-Hall.

1969c   "Fashion: From class differentiation to collective selection." *Sociological Quarterly* 10: 275–91.

1969d   *Symbolic Interactionism*. Englewood Cliffs, N.J.: Prentice-Hall.

1971   "Social problems as collective behavior." *Social Problems* 18: 298–306.

1972   "Action vs. interaction." *Society* 9: 50–53.

1973   "A note on symbolic interactionism." *American Sociological Review* 38: 797–98.

1977   "Comment on Lewis' 'The classic American pragmatists as forerunners to symbolic interactionism'." *Sociological Quarterly* 18: 285–9.

1978   "Social unrest and collective protest." In Norman K. Denzin (ed.), *Studies in Symbolic Interaction*, Vol. 1. Greenwich, Conn.: Jai Press, pp. 1–54.

1980   "Mead and Blumer: The convergent methodological perspectives of social behaviorism and symbolic interactionism." *American Sociological Review* 45: 409–419.

Other works cited

Apel, Karl-Otto, 1977. "The *a priori* of communication and the foundation of the humanities." In Fred R. Dallmayr and Thomas A. McCarthy (eds.), *Understanding and Social Inquiry*. Notre Dame, Ind.: University of Notre Dame Press.

Ayer, A.J. (ed.), 1959. *Logical Positivism*. New York: Free Press.

Becker, Howard S., 1953. "Becoming a marijuana user." *American Journal of Sociology* 59: 235–42.

Carnap, Rudolf, 1932. "The elimination of metaphysics through logical analysis of language" (translated by Arthur Pap). In A.J. Ayer (ed.), *Logical Positivism* (1959). New York: Free Press, pp. 60–81.

Dallmayr, Fred R., and Thomas A. McCarthy (eds.), 1977. *Understanding and Social Inquiry*. Notre Dame, Ind.: University of Notre Dame Press.

Feyerabend, Paul, 1975. *Against Method*. London: NLB.

Goffman, Erving, 1959. *The Presentation of Self in Everyday Life*. Garden City, N.J.: Doubleday.

Habermas, Jurgen, 1971. *Knowledge and Human Interests* (translated by Jeremy J. Shapiro). Boston: Beacon Press.

   1977. "A review of Gadamer's *Truth and Method*." In Fred R. Dallmayr and Thomas A. McCarthy (eds.), *Understanding and Social Inquiry*. Notre Dame, Ind.: University of Notre Dame Press, pp. 335–63.

Hanson, Norwood Russell, 1958. *Patterns of Discovery*. New York: Cambridge University Press.

Hempel, Carl G., 1950. "The empiricist criterion of meaning." In A.J. Ayer, *Logical Positivism* (1959). New York: Free Press, pp. 108–129.

Hesse, Mary, 1978. "Theory and value in the social sciences." In Christopher Hookway and Philip Pettit (eds.), *Action and Interpretation*. Cambridge: Cambridge University Press, pp. 1–16.

Husserl, Edmund, 1931. *Ideas* (translated by W.R. Boyce Gibson). New York: Collier.

   1970. *The Crisis of European Sciences and Transcendental Phenomenology* (translated by David Carr). Evanston, Ill.: Northwestern University Press.

Kant, Immanuel, 1965. *Critique of Pure Reason* (translated by Norman Kemp Smith). New York: St Martin's Press.

Klemke, E.D., Robert Hollinger, and A. David Kline (eds.), 1980. *Introductory Readings in the Philosophy of Science*. New York: Prometheus.

Korner, Stephan, 1970. *Categorial Frameworks*. New York: Barnes and Noble.

Leibniz, Gottfried Wilhelm Freiherr von, 1951. "Letter to Queen Charlotte of Prussia, 1702." In Philip P. Wiener (ed.), *Leibniz Selections*. New York: Scribner's, pp. 355–67.

McPhail, Clark, and Cynthia Rexroat, 1979. "Mead vs. Blumer: The divergent methodological perspectives of social behaviorism and symbolic interactionism." *American Sociological Review* 44: 449–67.

   1980. "*Ex cathedra* Blumer or *Ex libris* Mead?" *American Sociological Review* 45: 420–30.

Orcutt, James D., 1978. "Normative definitions of intoxicated states: A test of several sociological theories." *Social Problems* 25: 385–96.

Peirce, Charles Sanders, 1932. *Collected Papers*, Vol. 2 (edited by Charles Hartshorn and Paul Weiss). Cambridge, Mass.: Harvard University Press.

Plato, 1961. *Theaetetus* (translated by F.M. Cornford). In Edith Hamilton and Huntington Cairns (eds.), *The Collected Dialogues of Plato*. Princeton, N.J.: Princeton University Press.

Polanyi, Michael, 1962. *Personal Knowledge*. Chicago: University of Chicago Press.

Ricoeur, Paul, 1971. "The model of the text: Meaningful action considered as a text." In Paul Ricoeur, *Hermeneutics and the Human Sciences* (translated by John B. Thompson) (1981b). Cambridge: Cambridge University Press, pp. 145–64.

   1973. "Hermeneutics and the critique of ideology." In Paul Ricoeur, *Hermeneutics and the Human Sciences* (translated by John B. Thompson) (1981b). Cambridge: Cambridge University Press, pp. 63–100.

1974. "Science and ideology." In Paul Ricoeur, *Hermeneutics and the Human Sciences* (translated by John B. Thompson) (1981b). Cambridge: Cambridge University Press, pp. 222–46.

1975. "The hermeneutical function of distanciation." In Paul Ricoeur, *Hermeneutics and the Human Sciences* (translated by John B. Thompson) (1981b). Cambridge: Cambridge University Press, pp. 131–44.

1981a. "Appropriation." In Paul Ricoeur, *Hermeneutics and the Human Sciences* (translated by John B. Thompson) (1981b). Cambridge: Cambridge University Press, pp. 182–96.

1981b. *Hermeneutics and the Human Sciences* (translated by John B. Thompson). Cambridge: Cambridge University Press.

Sartre, Jean-Paul, 1956. *Being and Nothingness* (translated by Hazel E. Barnes). New York: Philosophical Library.

Suppe, Frederick, 1977. *The Structure of Scientific Theories*. Urbana, Ill.: University of Illinois Press.

Weber, Max, 1947. *The Theory of Social and Economic Organization* (translated by A.M. Henderson and Talcott Parsons). New York: Oxford University Press.

Woelfel, Joseph, 1967. "Comment on the Blumer–Bales dialogue concerning the interpretation of Mead's thought." *American Journal of Sociology* 72: 409.

Index

Other books in the series

J. Milton Yinger, Kiyoshi Ikeda, Frank Laycock, and Stephen J. Cutler: *Middle Start: An Experiment in the Educational Enrichment of Young Adolescents*

James A. Geschwender: *Class, Race, and Worker Insurgency: The League of Revolutionary Black Workers*

Paul Ritterband: *Education, Employment, and Migration: Israel in Comparative Perspective*

John Low-Beer: *Protest and Participation: The New Working Class in Italy*

Orrin E. Klapp: *Opening and Closing: Strategies of Information Adaptation in Society*

Rita James Simon: *Continuity and Change: A Study of Two Ethnic Communities in Israel*

Marshall B. Clinard: *Cities with Little Crime: The Case of Switzerland*

Steven T. Bossert: *Tasks and Social Relationships in Classrooms: A Study of Instructional Organization and Its Consequences*

Richard E. Johnson: *Juvenile Delinquency and Its Origins: An Integrated Theoretical Approach*

David R. Heise: *Understanding Events: Affect and the Construction of Social Action*

Ida Harper Simpson: *From Student to Nurse: A Longitudinal Study of Socialization*

Stephen P. Turner: *Sociological Explanation as Translation*

Janet W. Salaff: *Working Daughters of Hong Kong: Filial Piety or Power in the Family?*

Joseph Chamie: *Religion and Fertility: Arab Christian–Muslim Differentials*

William Friedland, Amy Barton, and Robert Thomas: *Manufacturing Green Gold: Capital, Labor, and Technology in the Lettuce Industry*

Richard N. Adams: *Paradoxical Harvest: Energy and Explanation in British History, 1870–1914*

Mary F. Rogers: *Sociology, Ethnomethodology, and Experience: A Phenomenological Critique*

James R. Beniger: *Trafficking in Drug Users: Professional Exchange Networks in the Control of Deviance*

Andrew J. Weigert, J. Smith Teitge, and Dennis W. Teitge: *Society and Identity: Toward a Sociological Psychology*

Jon Miller: *Pathways in the Workplace: The Effects of Gender and Race on Access to Organizational Resources*

Michael A. Fala: *Dynamic Functionalism: Strategy and Tactics*

Joyce Rothschild and J. Allen Whitt: *The Co-operative Workplace: Potentials and Dilemmas of Organizational Democracy*

Russell Thornton: *We Shall Live Again: The 1870 and 1890 Ghost Dance Movements as Demographic Revitalization*

Severyn T. Bruyn: *The Field of Social Investment*

Guy E. Swanson: *Ego Defenses and the Legitimation of Behaviour*

Liah Greenfeld: *Different Worlds: A Sociological Study of Taste, Choice and Success in Art*

Thomas K. Rudel: *Situations and Strategies in American Land-Use Planning*

Percy C. Hintzen: *The Costs of Regime Survival: Racial Mobilization, Elite Domination and Control of the State in Guyana and Trinidad*

John T. Flint: *Historical Role Analysis in the Study of Religious Change: Mass Educational Development in Norway, 1740–1891*

Judith R. Blau: *The Shape of Culture: A Study of Cultural Patterns in the United States*

Fred C. Pampel and John B. Williamson: *Age, Class, Politics and the Welfare State*

Thomas J. Fararo: *The Meaning of General Theoretical Sociology: Tradition and Formalization*

Lewis F. Carter: *Control and Charisma in Rajneeshpuram: The Role of Shared Values in the Creation of a Community*

David M. Heer: *Undocumented Mexicans in the United States*